CULTURAL
CONNECTIONS

Using literature to explore world cultures with children

Ron Jobe

Pembroke Publishers Limited

©1993 Pembroke Publishers
538 Hood Road
Markham, Ontario L3R 3K9

Canadian Cataloguing in Publication Data

Jobe, Ron
  Cultural connections : experiencing world literature
with children

Includes bibliographical references and index.
ISBN 1-55138-007-2

1. English literature – Study and teaching (Elementary).
I. Title.

LB1575.J63 1993   372.64′044   C93-094729-0

Editor: David Kilgour
Design: John Zehethofer
Cover Photography: Ajay Photographics
Typesetting: Jay Tee Graphics Ltd.

This book was produced with the generous assistance of the government
of Ontario through the Ministry of Culture and Communications.

Printed and bound in Canada by Webcom
9 8 7 6 5 4 3 2

Contents

Acknowledgements 5

Introduction 7

Chapter 1
Experiencing Literature with Children in a Global
Community 11

Chapter 2
Echoes of a Culture 16
　Our Heritage of Traditional Tales 16
　Encountering a Culture through Time Travel and Historical
　Fiction 25

Chapter 3
Experiencing the Themes of Cultural Literature 33
　Under the Surface: Cultural Encounters 34
　Entre Nous: Cross-Cultural Experiences 42
　Caught in the Shadow: Cultural Clashes 51
　The Rising Phoenix: Cultural Reawakenings 66

Chapter 4
Exploring the Cultural Literary Experience 76
　Cultural Voices 76
　　Key Books 9+ 78
　　　Onion Tears 78
　　　The Most Beautiful Place in the World 83
　　　Tikta'liktak 84
　　Key Books 10+ 87
　　　Number the Stars 87
　　　A Jar of Dreams 90
　　　Underground to Canada 93
　　Key Books 11+ 96
　　　Kiss the Dust 96
　　　Star Fisher 99
　　　The Curses of Third Uncle 103

The Eternal Spring of Mr. Ito   *105*
Homesick: My Own Story   *107*
Key Books 12+   *110*
Park's Quest   *110*
Shabanu   *114*
Year of Impossible Goodbyes   *122*
Cultural Voices in Translation   *126*
Cultural Visions   *128*

Chapter 5
Cultural Cross-Checks   *131*

Conclusion   *141*

Bibliography   *143*
Fiction   *143*
Picture Books   *147*
Folktales   *151*
Poetry   *154*
Publishing Acknowledgements   *155*

Acknowledgements

I would like to express my appreciation to all those colleagues, students, and friends who have expressed an interest in the evolution of this book.

I am especially indebted to Paula Hart, a wonderful colleague and friend, who helped to structure the book and gave helpful suggestions and editing assistance throughout the entire process.

It has always been my pleasure to have outstanding teachers as students in my classes, and I thank them for their response to many of the ideas and strategies in this book. A very special note of appreciation must go to a quartet of teachers who, as part of my class, became a reaction panel to the ideas in the book. Donna Beck, Nancy Fargey, Barbara Kay, and Donna Krawchuk were eager to participate and their enthusiasm for certain novels is evident in passages they wrote for the book.

Without fine colleagues where would we be? I particularly want to express my appreciation to Nirmal Bawa, Sally Clinton, and Jo-Anne Naslund for their editing skills and their refreshing encouragement.

I also want to acknowledge the assistance of Lee Ann Bryant of the UBC Education Library, Juliana Bayfield, president of IBBY Australia, and Betty Higdon of Reedley College in California for their contributions. I also appreciated the interest and expertise of the staff of two fine childrens' bookstores, The Bookery in Ottawa and Vancouver Kids Books.

Finally, a word of respect and appreciation for the many writers, illustrators, and translators mentioned in this book, for their caring about presenting cultural experiences for young people with a high degree of sensitivity, respect, and understanding. The time they took to care about the little details shows in the titles recommended here.

Introduction

The structure for this book was designed with Paula Hart based on the feedback we received to *Canadian Connections*. Response indicated the need for further approaches to interacting with literature, particularly literature that reflects the changing cultural reality to be found in classrooms.

This book is designed to be a sharing with teachers and librarians who already have a good general knowledge of children's books, but who want to be challenged to think in new directions, to enhance their own awareness and appreciation of literature, and to achieve a heightened sensitivity to their own culture and that of others.

A* is a symbol that stands for ACTIVE approaches on the part of students and teachers. These are planned to suggest, stimulate, and point out new directions. They are designed to appeal to many ages, from intermediate students to 'intermediate' age teachers! We, as teachers, gain more insight into our culture and the culture of others by engaging directly in the activities and reflecting on major questions.

As educators, we must continue to strive to place increased emphasis on similarities among cultures. What do we share in common? As president of IBBY, the International Board on Books for Young People, I have had the opportunity to visit educators, writers, illustrators, translators, and children's literature centres in many parts of the world. Everywhere, people are interested in sharing the best of their children's books with others and in finding out what youngsters in other countries are reading. To make our students aware of other people around the world is an important mission for educators. Thus, I recommend you look at a list of the winners of the Batchelder Award (US), given for the best translations into English each year, and IBBY's Hans

Christian Andersen Award. The latter award, given every two years, is considered to be the most prestigious in the world.

Using This Book

I would like to invite you and your students to approach literature in a new way. Always read first to enjoy a book, but also read with a cultural perspective in mind. Then, take time to sit quietly and reflect. I like to have a pad of paper to jot down thoughts and activities which come to mind. If you make time for this reflection, you'll find that not only will you have a clearer recall of the novel, but you will have begun to make valuable connections between the book and your own experiences.

Chapter 1, "Experiencing Literature with Children in a Global Community," explains the importance of students having cultural literary experiences as part of their lives. I start by noting that students come to school with culture and are in the process of evolving their own cultural identity as they broaden their experience in school and the community. All of us get our initial sense of culture by looking at our own lives first.

Chapter 2, "Echoes of a Culture," offers a means to introduce students to cultural experiences. The vast majority of so-called 'multicultural' titles appearing in bibliographies are folktales. They are important aspects of our cultural heritage from the past, and if we become aware of them they will become part of our own personal culture. There is a danger that they may be interpreted as being too 'old' and having no relevance for today's students. We, as teachers, must present them in a way that brings out the links to the present and to all our lives. Through the use of time travel and historical fiction we enable students to become active observers, almost going within the setting to join the characters. I suppose it is the exotic appeal of the past that heightens their awareness and observation, yet it can lead to a lasting impression on young minds.

Chapter 3, "Experiencing the Themes of Cultural Literature," looks at concepts and books that are related thematically. It includes approaches and activities which link the issues within each cultural thematic unit. The major purpose is always to strengthen books' cultural connections.

Chapter 4, "Exploring the Cultural Literary Experience," presents novels and picture books which offer rich reading experiences for students.

The "Key Books" are the very special ones. They have been arranged by the four intermediate age groups (9+,10+,11+,12+) for ease of selection. It should be remembered that the maturity of readers and their past experiences will affect the appropriateness of each title. In this chapter three or more titles are explored in detail at each age level, with a synopsis of the story followed by a variety of approaches considered appropriate for it. A section on voices in translation gives an introduction to some of the fine literature being translated into English. Exciting for me has been the voluntary contribution of several practicing teachers. As a teacher or librarian you should be regularly sharing your own adult reading with the students. Why not read favorite passages from such titles as Joy Kogawa's *Obasan* or Amy Tan's *The Joy Luck Club* and *The Kitchen God's Wife*?

"Cultural Visions" includes those picture book titles which offer a unique cultural experience appropriate for the intermediate student. Increasingly, picture books are being designed for an older reader, as evidenced by the myriad of details and complexity of text. I have included many picture books because they have a major role to play in giving culture an identity, not just in terms of humanity but of setting, mood, and tradition. It is always a source of surprise and delight to see students become aware of cultural details in the illustrations.

Chapter 5, "Cultural Cross-Checks," offers a response to the question, "How do I know if this is an accurate portrayal of a culture?" It also includes responses to cultural content by people of the culture represented. I have included a guide to help you do your own cross-checking with your students in their consideration of the cultural aspects of a book.

Throughout the book, 'reflections' encourage teachers and librarians to think about the depth and richness of cultural experiences shared with children and to open up some new directions.

The most appropriate way to conclude a book on the topic of literature for young people is with a listing of those titles I have selected as being most appropriate for any intermediate literature-based program. The bibliography is not meant to be an all-inclusive list; rather it is a selective guide introducing cultural literary experiences. With time and confidence, you will find stories of your own to treasure and share with others.

Chapter 1

Experiencing Literature with Children in a Global Community

Each child reader brings to the reading of a book his or her own experiential background, family heritage, and the pressures of mass culture. Literature offers student readers a cultural experience that extends and enriches their lives. It can introduce them to different cultures, raising their awareness of other people. The emphasis must always be on an accurate and respectful portrayal, quality literature, and good illustration.

Students come to the classroom rich in their own culture. We as teachers must recognize this resource in our students but also see the necessity to encourage them to reflect on their own developing culture. What are the cultural influences on students today? Like no other previous generation, our students receive an almost overwhelming bombardment of cultural impressions. The conscious and unconscious reception of these forms their views and determines their outlook on people, issues, and happenings. One thing literature does for us is to make us realize that culture is not always exotic; more than likely it is shown in the everyday occurrences we all share.

In a Cultural Bubble

A* To encourage students to reflect on the extent of this cultural bombardment, have them, in small groups, imagine that they are enclosed in a large bubble. This sphere represents their world. From the inside they look out and see the various pressures, influences, and demands on them. Are they aware of them? Where are these coming from? How much control do they have? Ask each group to make a model with themselves in the centre, writing the type of pressure/influence on them around the outside. The stronger the pressure/influence the closer to the bubble, the lesser the further away. Each group can then

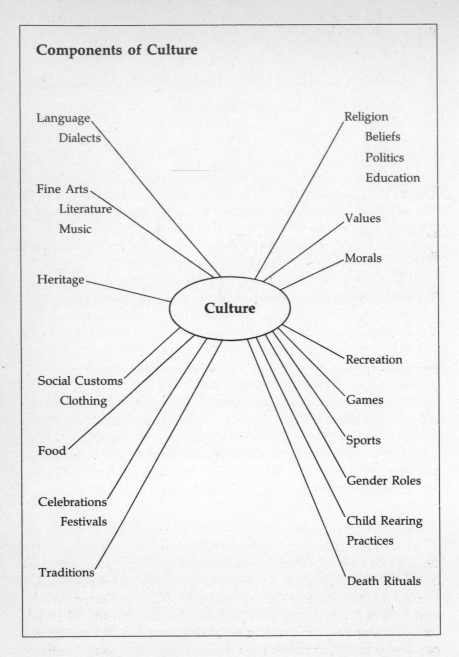

Components of Culture

Language
Dialects

Fine Arts
Literature
Music

Heritage

Social Customs
Clothing

Food

Celebrations
Festivals

Traditions

Culture

Religion
Beliefs
Politics
Education

Values

Morals

Recreation

Games

Sports

Gender Roles

Child Rearing
Practices

Death Rituals

illustrate with both words and images the cultural influences on them. Pictures from magazines and newspaper headlines can be used to create a very effective montage of influences.

The following model gives a visual representation of some of these cultural influences on students.

The Student's World

Cultural Background
— role models
— values
— foods
— clothing

Student's Wants
— talents

Learning Styles

Recreation
— involved or not

Student's Health
— special needs
— challenges

Economy
— socioeconomic level

Politics

Religion

Daycare

Teachers

Media

Advertisements

Peer Groups

Peer Pressure

Exposure to Literature

Family Influence
— changing family roles
— values
— role models
— siblings

An activity such as this helps students to become more aware of what is meant by the term culture. Basically, culture is a term used to describe a unique set of customs, languages, religious beliefs, attitudes, and behaviors shared by a group of people and passed on from generation to generation. These collective beliefs and values provide members with a sense of identity. But culture also implies communication and a means to communicate, because it is only through the transmission of a group's culture that a sense of group identity and tradition evolves. And, of course, children have their own lore—the language they speak among themselves, their popular expressions, games, schoolground myths, how they establish a pecking order in a group, etc.

Children in a Global Community

The changing face of the modern classroom reflects the fact that because of immigration, we have become a multicultural society. Students will have to become more aware of this in order to effectively live and operate within such a community. What can we expect of our students as global citizens?
- They will have a high degree of cultural awareness.
- They will be multilingual with a desire to read books in several languages.
- They will be sensitive to and accepting of others.
- They will be discriminating consumers in the mass markets of the world.

Literature allows us to see our own culture and to experience the culture of others in a way we cannot do in our daily life. To heighten an awareness of the role of literature, I like to pose the following questions to teachers in my multicultural children's literature course at the beginning and ending of each term. They have relevance for you as you read this book. Consider them before, during, and after your reading.

- What universal constants among cultures are portrayed in children's books?
- In what ways are children's books a reflection of the society in which they were written?
- What benefits are gained by children when they read cross-cultural literature?
- What is the importance to the self-concept of children in being able to recognize themselves in cross-cultural literature?
- How can the authenticity of a culture portrayed in literature for children be assessed?
- Do countries have literary mosaics? What is the image of Canada (or any country/culture) in children's books? Which books could help recent immigrants to learn about Canada and its people?
- What is the relevance of the comment made by Janet Lunn, "No country is ever settled just once. Each new generation must settle it again in their imaginations"?

- Why is it important for educators to go beyond the traditional "F" approach to multiculturalism (Food, Festivals, Folklore, Fun), and how can literature enrich multicultural understanding and experience?

Chapter 2

Echoes of a Culture

Internationally respected translator Edward Fenton has commented that his role in translating a work of historical fiction is actually to present the echoes of the past. What a remarkable concept! An echo reflects sound back—or more precisely gives back what is already there. So, too, our culture reflects the echoes of an earlier time.

As professional educators we need to ask how we can interest our students in finding out about the cultures of the past. For starters, we can share our heritage through traditional tales and through time travel/historical fiction.

Our Heritage of Traditional Tales

Traditional tales preserve cultural beliefs, morality, and contextual factors such as settings, foods, and customs. Current publishing trends have resulted in an increase in the number of individual folktales being produced, a response to consumer demands for more multicultural materials. Sadly, although these tales come from different countries there is an inherent danger that unless they are interpreted in an appropriate manner, they may give youngsters a sense that all are set in the past and therefore have no relevance to our lives today. And yet these tales give children of all backgrounds a chance to discover their own heritage and to take pride in their roots. They also provide an opportunity for children who have different backgrounds to become aware of aspects of their friends' cultures. It is important for students to have an appreciation for how similar their folktale roots really are.

History may give us the facts, but it is folktales that let us know how people feel or what is important to them. Thus these traditional tales must be presented not as relics of the past but rather as dynamic, ever-changing stories with relevance to our lives.

Traditional Folktales

Every country has a long heritage of folktales. 'Old World' countries, both East and West, are full of tales which have been told and handed down for countless generations. As members of a culture move away from their homeland, one of the most important things they take with them, in either oral or written form, is the cumulative memory of these tales.

There are so many tales readily available that a stimulating way of sharing them with students is to have a flood of books in the classroom. Challenge the students to conduct an 'undercover' **FT** (folktale) **RAID** on the school library resource centre to capture as many different illustrated tales as they can. Then, sitting comfortably in the midst of these books, allow students time to read any number of them.

A* "Cultural Detectives:" Encourage students to become cultural detectives. Groups of two or three students could search in their homes and at the public library for well-illustrated adult references on the arts and cultures represented in the books, hunting for proof that some of the objects portrayed in the illustrations are real, their designs authentic, the coloration exact, the clothing precise, etc. When a book has been examined by several groups, a comparative sharing could be given in class. What evidence did each group find of the culture? Were there any differences?

The value of this activity is in the sharing and comparing nature of the discussion which takes place about the illustrations and the story; the final result is certainly an enhanced ability to detect cultural attributes. Reading and sharing the following sampler of folktales representing many cultures will help reveal our global heritage.

Aardema, Verna. *Why Mosquitoes Buzz in People's Ears*. Illustrated by Leo and Diane Dillon. When a mosquito whispers something in an iguana's ear, a surprising chain reaction takes place in the west African jungle.

Bailey, Lydia. *Mei Ming and the Dragon's Daughter*. Illustrated by Martin Springett. When drought affects her people, a young

Chinese girl realizes she must go up the mountain and release the water in a large lake, but it is guarded by a ferocious dragon.

Cleaver, Elizabeth. *The Enchanted Caribou*. Through the medium of shadow puppets an Inuit woman is tricked by a shaman and becomes a white caribou.

Compton, Patricia A. (reteller). *The Terrible EEK*. Illustrated by Sheila Hamanaka. A Japanese father admits to being afraid of the EEK, just as a robber and a wolf overhear him. When the robber falls off the roof onto the wolf both think the EEK has arrived—setting off a hilarious chain of events.

Goble, Paul. *Love Flute*. A young Santee Dakota man too shy to tell a beautiful girl he is in love with her leaves the village, and one night receives a special gift from the animals to help him.

Hearn, Lafcadio. *The Voice of the Great Bell*. Retold by Margaret Hodges. Illustrated by Ed Young. When the Emperor of China demands a bell be made which can be heard for a hundred miles, it takes a young girl to give her life to save her father.

Heyer, Marilee. *The Weaving of a Dream*. When a Chinese widow, who weaves magnificent brocades, copies one from a special painting and loses it to the wind, she sends in turn her three sons to retrieve it.

Hughes, Monica. *Little Fingerling*. Illustrated by Brenda Clark. When he is fifteen years old, and still only one finger tall, a young Japanese boy, Issun Boshi, sets off to see the world and find his fortune.

Ishii, Momoko (reteller). *The Tongue-cut Sparrow*. Illustrated by Suekichi Akaba. Translated from the Japanese by Katherine Paterson. A kind old man and his greedy wife receive appropriate gifts from a sparrow.

Johnson, Ryerson. *Kenji and the Magic Geese*. Illustrated by Jean and Mou-sien Tseng. When only four geese appear on a painting instead of the original five, a young boy goes to investigate.

Louie, Ai-Ling (reteller). *Yeh-Shen; A Cinderella Story from China*. Illustrated by Ed Young.

Martin, Rafe. *The Rough-Face Girl*. Illustrated by David Shannon. An Algonquin Cinderella story.

Mollel, Tololwa M. *The King and the Tortoise*. Illustrated by Kathy Blankley. A retelling of the Cameroon tale determining who is the most clever animal of all. Illustrated with traditional Cameroon designs.

Mollel, Tololwa M. *The Orphan Boy*. Illustrated by Paul Morin. Who is the strange boy who wanders into the Masai village?

Morris, Winifred. *The Future of Yen-Tzu*. Illustrated by Friso Henstra. The youngest son of a Chinese farmer sets out to find a better future, only to find that it keeps changing.

San Souci, Robert D. *Sukey and the Mermaid*. Illustrated by Brian Pinkney. An African-American tale of an unusual friendship on an island off the coast of South Carolina.

Steptoe, John. *Mufaro's Beautiful Daughters*. Two sisters in Zimbabwe seek to marry the Great King.

Steptoe, John. *The Story of Jumping Mouse; A Native American Legend*. Black and white illustrations dramatize the generosity of a small rodent.

Toye, William (reteller). *How Summer Came to Canada*. Illustrated by Elizabeth Cleaver. A collage interpretation of the agreement between summer and winter to share Glooskap's land.

Toye, William (reteller). *The Loon's Necklace*. Illustrated by Elizabeth Cleaver. Helping an old Tsimshian man to regain his sight, loon is given his shell necklace, a gift which leaves its distinctive markings.

Toye, William (reteller). *The Mountain Goats of Temlaham*. Illustrated by Elizabeth Cleaver. The kindness of a Tsimshian boy towards a young mountain goat is repaid in full.

Watkins, Yoko Kawashima. *Tales from the Bamboo Grove*. Illustrations by Jean and Mou-sien Tseng. Six tales remembered from a Japanese childhood.

Yacowitz, Caryn (adaptor). *The Jade Stone; A Chinese Folktale*. Illustrated by Ju-Hong Chen. At the Chinese emperor's urging, a lowly stone carver starts to carve a magnificent dragon, but the stone dictates that a trio of carp should emerge instead.

Yolen, Jane. *The Emperor and the Kite*. Illustrated by Ed Young. Imprisoned in a tall tower, a Chinese emperor is aided by the daughter he had previously ignored, when she designs a kite to help. Intricate paper cut technique illustrations.

COLLECTIONS

Hamilton, Virginia. *The Dark Way, Stories from the Spirit World*. Illustrated by Lambert Davis.

Rosen, Michael. *How the Animals Got Their Colors*. Illustrated by John Clementson.

Te Kanawa, Kiri. *Land of the Long White Cloud; Maori Myths, Tales and Legends*. Illustrated by Michael Foreman.

Vuong, Lynette Dyer. *The Brocaded Slipper and Other Vietnamese Tales*. Illustrated by Vo-Dinh Mai.

Transported Tales

These are traditional tales which have been brought from somewhere else. The settings have been changed to the new locations to which people have moved. Most often the stories remain essentially the same but are fleshed out with details about the new settings.

Bang, Mollie. *Dawn*. A moving tale, taken from the Japanese, of a beautiful woman with wondrous weaving skills, is set in 19th-century New England.

Harris, Joel Chandler. *Jump Again! More Adventures of Brer Rabbit*. Adapted by Van Dyke Parks. Illustrated by Barry Moser. Stories about a rabbit whose resourcefulness and courage can overcome any odds.

Jaquith, Priscilla (reteller). *Bo Rabbit Smart for True; Folktales from the Gullah*. Drawings by Ed Young. A quartet of hilarious tales drawn from an African heritage but told within an American context.

Spray, Carole. *The Mare's Egg; A New World Folktale*. Illustrated by Kim LaFave. An amusing tale of a pioneer simpleton who is tricked into believing that a mare will hatch out of a pumpkin.

Transformed Tales

These are traditional stories which people have transplanted not only to a new setting but also to a new culture. They are different from the originals, but within them we still see respect for traditional motifs and cultural attitudes. There is respect for the dead, for ancestors, and for family unity. A splendid example of a transformed tale is the movie *Star Wars*, which is based on Norse myths.

Hamilton, Virginia. *The All Jahdu Storybook*. ''Now begins the time of the magic trickster, Jahdu." A series of tales about this famous trickster, set in America today.

Hamilton, Virginia (reteller). *The People Could Fly; American Black Folktales*. Illustrated by Leo and Diane Dillon. Based on the stories the slaves brought with them from Africa, a collection of tales which evolved on southern plantations.

Hooks, William H. *Moss Gown*. Illustrated by Donald Carrick. A traditional southern tale of a young girl, banished by her father and sisters, being helped by a green-eyed witch woman. She gives her a wonderful dress to go to the ball. Elements of King Lear and Cinderella are woven into the telling.

Muller, Robin. *The Magic Paintbrush*. Set in pre-industrial Europe, this retelling of a Chinese folktale is the story of a young orphan who is given a special brush that makes his paintings come to life. The greedy king demands more and more until Nibs throws the paints into the sea.

Yee, Paul. *Tales from Gold Mountain; Stories of the Chinese in the New World*. Illustrated by Simon Ng. Eight stories set in Canada but based on traditions brought from China.

Embedded Tales

These are tales within other works of literature. Writers place references to folktales within their work to give a sense of continuity with the past, to carry on the cultural traditions important to the characters, to add a level of metaphor or a sense of magic.

Students will have experienced such embedded stories when visiting grandparents or other relatives have, in the course of conversation, lapsed into a story. These could be family stories relating to specific incidents, events which have become part of the family legend, or stories told them by their own grandparents. What better way to realize just how stories are passed on from one generation to the next? This happens in Amy Tan's *The Moon Lady*, when a Chinese grandmother tells young girls a story about her youth.

Other such tales are found in the following:

Drucker, Malka. *Grandma's Latkes* by Malka Drucker. Illustrated by Eve Chwast. A young girl is selected to help her grandmother make potato pancakes, a feature of Hanukkah celebrations. During the preparations she learns how Judah Macca-bee miraculously defeated the Roman Antiochus so that the Jewish people could survive.

Grifalconi, Ann. *The Village of Round and Square Houses*. A young girl wonders why her village with its style of houses looks like no other. Late one evening, after she has had a last puff of her pipe, Gran'ma Tika sits back and tells her the tale.

Hunter, Mollie. *A Stranger Came Ashore*. A young boy living on a Scottish island is puzzled by the strange smile of a young man who arrived during a severe storm. It is only when his grandfather recalls tales of the Selkie Folk that the frighten-ing truth is revealed about Finn Learson.

Joseph, Lynn. *A Wave in Her Pocket: Stories from Trinidad*. A young girl, Amber, tells of her wonderful grand aunt Tantie who knows a story for every occasion.

Yep, Laurence. *Star Fisher*. Joan is the eldest of three children of a Chinese-American family who are the first of Chinese descent to arrive in a small town in West Viriginia. She tells her younger sister the story of the golden Kingfisher maiden who was forced to marry the man who had hidden her golden cloak and thus prevented her return to her sisters in the sky. Later she relates her feelings of loneliness and rejection in the town where nobody wants her, to the feelings of the starfisher.

Fractured Tales

These include basic elements of the originals (language, setting, characters, events), but so strikingly changed that their impact is humorous. Amusing interpretations, adaptations, and exten-sions of traditional tales are part of cultural reality and give evi-dence of the fact that culture evolves. Increasingly, folktales are published which shift emphasis, change characters or make a complete turn-around in theme.

Do these modern interpretations destroy the traditional tales? No! When written well, they make the traditional motifs stand out even more clearly.

The concern of the writers of fractured tales is that we so often pass our tales down through static writing and traditional vis-ual images that the telling is not alive or dynamic. These tellers want to tease children, as do Jean Little and Maggie DeVries in *Once upon a Golden Apple*. They invite children to recognize the traditional references and chuckle with delight at amusing changes. The chief appeal is that they are funny!

The following are some well-known fractures.

Dahl, Roald. *Roald Dahl's Revolting Rhymes*. Illustrated by Quentin Blake.

French, Fiona. *Snow White in New York*. At home with gangsters in the 1920s.

Hewitt, Kathryn (reteller). *The Three Sillies*. The sweetheart of the farmer's daughter sets off on a journey to find three bigger sillies. Amusing pig characters transpose traditional scenes with modern tourist trips.

Little, Jean, and Maggie DeVries. *Once upon a Golden Apple*. A father teases his children with wrong details in this mock fairy tale.

Perlman, Janet (reteller & adaptor). *Cinderella Penguin, or, The Little Glass Flipper*. Caught under the trap door when the Prince's footmen come, the glass flipper just happens to fall on Cinderella's foot!

Scieszka, Jon. *The Frog Prince Continued*. Paintings by Steve Johnson. And they lived happily ever after—don't count on it! Bad habits follow us through life especially if they are like the Prince's irritating froggy habits.

Scieszka, Jon. *The Stinky Cheese Man: And Other Fairly Stupid Tales*. Illustrated by Lane Smith. Be prepared!

Scieszka, Jon. *The True Story of the Three Little Pigs* by A. Wolf. Illustrated by Lane Smith. Falsely accused of a terrible deed, Mr. Wolf has his turn to tell what really happened.

Stevens, Janet (reteller). *The Three Billy Goats Gruff*. A visual twist puts the older goat into dark glasses and leather jacket to frighten off the terrible troll.

Insights into a Culture

Encourage students to examine each cultural tale or historical setting and identify the markers which give insights into the culture. Using the points that follow will guide their exploration, focusing their attention on significant factors.

A. Visual Markers of Culture

1. **Visible Indicators**
   a. personal
      - dress, costume, jewelry
      - food
      - artifacts, tools
      - activities

   b. setting
      - landscapes
      - famous landmarks
      - buildings, houses, markets

2. **Implied Indicators**
   a. cultural indicators
      - color
      - design, patterns
      - objects
      - places
      - characters

   b. cultural attitudes
      - posture
      - position
      - values
      - respect
      - social conventions
      - generational indicators
      - gender indicators

B. Language Markers of Culture

1. **Language Patterns**
   a. names
      - princess, sultan

   b. specific expressions
      - words, phrases, chants

   c. dialogue patterns

   d. storytelling patterns (rhythm, onomatopoeia)

2. **Narrative Patterns**
   a. traditional opening phrase

   b. story type
   - beast
   - cumulative
   - formula
   - hero
   - initiation
   - journey
   - noodle head
   - pourquoi
   - realistic
   - trickster
   - wonder

   c. story structure
   - pattern of three (wishes, objects, etc.)
   - description, long prologue

   d. traditional conclusion

Reflection:

History books may give us facts, but tales let us know how people feel, and thus students may become more aware of their cultural heritage.

In comparing folktales from many cultures, one notices that people share common needs: we have an apparent need to unravel mysteries, to explain unusual phenomena, to seek justice and order and to delight in life.

Encountering a Culture through Time Travel and Historical Fiction

The genre of time travel offers a unique challenge to an author to present a duality of cultural experiences as well as to tell a story in two time periods. This offers readers as well as writers the chance to undertake extensive comparative cultural research, identifying areas of cultural compatibility, similarity, and difference.

Details of daily life in the past might be explored.

- What was life really like for people living then?
- If you were living then what would it be like for you?
- What might be your daily schedule?
- What smells might you notice?
- What sights would you see and what do you think you might encounter just around the corner?
- Who might be your friends?
- How would you make friends?
- How would you survive?
- When you got hungry what would you do?
- What would bring you happiness?

As characters travel in time, they usually take with them their own sensibilities and standards. The effect this has on them and on the people they meet in their new environment is part of the intrigue. Janet Lunn, in *The Root Cellar*, makes the time period accessible to the reader by showing it through the eyes of the main character. Imagine Rose's surprise when she is taken for a boy because she is wearing jeans and a T-shirt, not the hoop skirts, bonnets, and petticoats of the time she goes back to.

As characters encounter the contact culture, students will be able to assess and discuss each individual's preparedness for the adventure. How do the characters grow in their appreciation for the culture of others?

- How do they realize that they have arrived in a different location and different culture?
- Who do they meet first?
- What cultural indicators do their contacts reveal (speech, clothing, references, etc.)?
- After fear often comes hunger—what will time travellers eat first? How familiar will this be for them, and what will it signal about the contact culture?
- How will they survive?
- How do they feel about leaving behind friends and loved ones in both time periods?
- Do they feel homesick? Could this be how immigrant families feel?
- What is it they miss most about their home, friends, and family?

Travellers in Time

Age	
9+	*Garth and the Mermaid* by Barbara Smucker

Age	
10+	*Who Is Frances Rain?* by Margaret Buffie
	The Doll by Cora Taylor
	The Devil's Arithmetic by Jane Yolen

Age	
11+	*The Root Cellar* by Janet Lunn
	Tom's Midnight Garden by Philippa Pearce

Age	
12+	*A Further Shore* by Nancy Bond
	Playing Beattie Bow by Ruth Park

One way to heighten students' awareness of what it is like to be in a different society, with different customs, values, and outlook, is to read aloud a time travel novel to the class, experiencing along with the characters and the students another time and place. During the reading emphasis should be placed on the observations of the characters as detected by the students. Details of daily life can be discussed and researched. Reference books, photographs, and literary accounts can be used to heighten the interest along with a comprehension of the pressures on the characters.

Keeping this in mind we can examine culture in a scientific way, emulating the approach of anthropologists.

Another intriguing and inspiring way to get students involved in another culture is to read a fine work (carefully selected) of historical fiction to them. Teachers frequently fall into the trap of thinking that skills sessions are more important, but in the long-term view, the oral reading of a pertinent novel is more significant than rote drills.

Echoes of the Past

Age	
9+	*Bells of Christmas* by Virginia Hamilton
	The Lamplighter by Bernice Thurman Hunter
	Sarah Plain and Tall by Patricia MacLachlan
	The Whipping Boy by Sid Fleischman

10+   *I Am David* by Anne Holm
      Adam of the Road by Elizabeth Janet Gray
      A Jar of Dreams by Yoshiko Uchida

11+   *The Eternal Spring of Mr. Ito* by Sheila Garrigue
      A Parcel of Patterns by Jill Paton Walsh
      Sweetgrass by Jan Hudson
      The True Confessions of Charlotte Doyle by Avi
      The Witch of Blackbird Pond by Elizabeth Speare

12+   *Lyddie* by Katherine Paterson
      December Rose by Leon Garfield
      Shadow in Hawthorn Bay by Janet Lunn
      Stepping on the Cracks by Mary Hahn
      Frank Thompson: Her Civil War Story by Bryna Stevens

Authors of historical fiction spend many hours researching a time period, focusing on customs, food, politics, religion, morals, language, and daily activities in order to present a story woven within the fabric of a society differing from our own. They create a dynamic cultural microcosm which the reader is able to observe and experience.

A*   As they read a novel, teachers should allow themselves the luxury (actually a necessity) of a relaxed reading pace accompanied by a willingness to let what happens happen. There is no need to rush through the book. It is important to be a fellow traveller in time with the characters and the students. Consider the following titles:

Avi. *The True Confessions of Charlotte Doyle*. Who was to know that boarding the brig destined for Providence on June 16, 1832 would have such an effect on a girl's life?

Fleischman, Sid. *The Whipping Boy*. Illustrations by Peter Sis. Life for a poor orphan was one whipping after another, especially when the prince for whom he had to receive punishment was a brat.

Garfield, Leon. *December Rose*. A mystery set in Victorian London.

Garrigue, Sheila. *The Eternal Spring of Mr. Ito*. Life for a gentle Japanese gardener in Vancouver changes following the bombing of Pearl Harbor.

Gray, Elizabeth Janet. *Adam of the Road*. Illustrated by Robert

Lawson. Life in 13th-century England seen through the eyes of a minstrel's son.

Hahn, Mary Downing. *Stepping on the Cracks*. Two girls living in a small town during World War II are confronted by the loss of a brother and desertion from the army.

Hamilton, Virginia. *Bells of Christmas*. Illustrated by Lambert Davis. The joy of an Ohio black family celebrating their 1890 Christmas.

Holm, Anne. *I Am David*. Translated from the Danish by L. W. Kingsland. A young boy in a prison camp is allowed to escape to his freedom and his rediscovery of the world.

Hudson, Jan. *Sweetgrass*. A teenage Blackfoot girl living in the 1890s must deal with a tribal raid, a harsh winter, and smallpox.

Hunter, Bernice Thurman. *The Lamplighter*. A story of childhood in the 1880s in Ontario.

Lunn, Janet. *Shadow in Hawthorn Bay*. Arriving in Upper Canada, a young Scottish girl struggles with pioneer life.

MacLachlan, Patricia. *Sarah Plain and Tall*. A mail-order bride arrives to join a prairie family.

Paterson, Katherine. *Lyddie*. A farm girl goes to work in the textile mills in Lowell, Massachusetts in the 1840s.

Speare, Elizabeth George. *The Witch of Blackbird Pond*. Becoming friends with an old Quaker woman is not approved of by the Puritans in a small Connecticut town.

Stevens, Bryna. *Frank Thompson: Her Civil War Story*. How was it that a Canadian woman was able to join the Union forces in the Civil War as a soldier?

Uchida, Yoshiko. *A Jar of Dreams*. It was tough to be a Japanese-American living in California during the depression.

Walsh, Jill Paton. *A Parcel of Patterns*. The plague arrives from London, along with the patterns being used to cut woven cloth.

The sharing of a novel set in a historical period can present a perspective on the multi-layered nature of life. Excellent examples to read aloud including the two following titles.

The Witch of Blackbird Pond

Elizabeth George Speare

When Barbadian teenager Kit Tyler arrives in 19th-century New England she is in for a shock. Rather than being part of the gentry she now must stay with her Puritan aunt and uncle and work on the farm with her cousins. It is a hard life. They have to raise their food, make their clothes and even their own candles. The drab life brought about by the hardships of daily living is accompanied by a strict, intolerant religious fervor. The Puritans are scripture-focused and look for evil in each person rather than positive qualities.

Kit, always headstrong, goes against her uncle's wishes and befriends an old Quaker woman and a little girl who is physically abused by her mother. Old Hannah becomes a source of friendship and support for Kit. Alas, when children in the town start dying the Puritan elders blame it on this very friendship—they must be witches! Kit helps Hannah to escape, but is herself imprisoned and put on trial.

When reading this novel aloud to a group of students take time to pause at the end of each reading and find out what you have all learned from the section.

A* Challenge the students: like Kit, they are going to be sent to a Puritan farm, and as they listen to the story they should be accumulating the facts they will need to know for their survival. They should also try to get a sense of the place and the people.

Construct a chart of the following:

The Culture at Blackbird Pond

Basic needs (food, clothing, shelter)
Religious beliefs
Laws
Education
Family structure
Role of children

A* If students could take only one thing with them to help them in their plight, what would it be?

Stepping on the Cracks
Mary Downing Hahn

In her powerful novel, Hahn provides us with a different kind of cultural time capsule. World War II is seen through the eyes of two eleven-year-old American girls, Margaret and Elizabeth, in Maryland. Although it seems far away, the war certainly impinges on their lives.

> It was Hitler's fault my brother Jimmy was in the army, Hitler's fault Mother cried when she thought I couldn't hear, Hitler's fault Daddy never laughed or told jokes, Hitler's fault, Hitler's fault, Hitler's most horrible fault. I hated him and his Nazis with a passion so strong and deep it scared me.

In an interesting parallel development, the girls' lives are not peaceful within; they have a town bully, Gordy Smith, to contend with.

The daily life of the girls is splendidly portrayed in this novel. Some teachers may be amazed at the flood of memories that will come forth as they read this book aloud.

A* Encourage the students to collect examples of the culture of the '40s mentioned in the book. Many may have videos or tapes of old movies, radio shows, or hit music. What fun it is for people of all ages to listen to episodes of "The Lone Ranger" and "The Shadow." Reproductions of magazines, comics, and newspapers can also be obtained. The idea is to make the time and culture come alive for the students.

Ask parents or grandparents for their memories of the times. Perhaps a 1944 "museum" corner could be established in the classroom, with items brought in from home.

As the war progresses, the girls have to face continued bullying by Gordy, but more importantly the death of Margaret's brother, Jimmy.

It is a very sad time, yet they also realize that other things are happening in their community. Gordy is being beaten at home by his father, explaining some of his anger, and his brother, a deserter and conscientious objector, lies very ill in a hut in the wood.

What should the girls do? A stimulating question to have students tackle.

Hahn addresses the issue of desertion from patriotic forces. Set as it is within a strong cultural portrait, her story will give students much food for thought.

Reflection:

The sharing of a novel set in a historical period can present the multi-layered nature of life, helping us to realize that our needs, hopes, and desires were relevant for people in past societies.

Sharing historical fiction gives a vehicle by which to become more aware of what culture is all about. By seeing the impact of culture on a past society, we are better able to become aware of our culture, and how it influences our lives within it. It allows us to respond to such questions as the following:

What is a distinctive culture?
What are the constants in culture?
How can we accurately observe a culture?
How do we identify cultural artifacts?
What are examples of cultural overgeneralizations?

The focus of our endeavors should be to find what we admire in a culture and the influence of its folklore.

Chapter 3

Experiencing the Themes of Cultural Literature

A major part of any approach to literature or indeed multiculturalism should be to place greater emphasis on the commonalities and similarities among peoples rather than on their differences.

Four major themes have been chosen for this book, each linking to the others in many ways. The first considers cultural encounters. It is a known fact that we make many judgements about people we meet within thirty seconds, based on what we see on the surface. In this chapter we will consider what goes on under the surface, where so many of our emotions, opinions, and cultural habits lie. "Entre Nous" investigates what happens when we get to know someone from a culture better through cross-cultural experiences. Since not all cultural encounters are positive, clashes often erupt. This will become evident in "Caught in the Shadow," which is about how it feels to be overwhelmed by another power. Happily, there has been an exciting revival of interest in the cultures of many groups all over the world. We will examine some of these in the final thematic unit, "The Rising Phoenix."

Teachers should take time to explore these themes with their students, allowing everyone time to explore their own thoughts, to expand horizons, integrate ideas, rethink, and reflect on their experiences.

Encourage yourself and your students to read the many recommended titles in this book, making certain that you provide time for sharing and reflecting on how each one relates to the theme in question and to each other.

This approach allows you as the teacher to be an equal participant in the exploration of each theme. It gives you intellectual stimulation and an appreciation for the ideas and abilities of your students. It is important to realize that teachers need just as much stimulation, interest, and reward as students.

Under the Surface: Cultural Encounters

Most of us are aware of our own habits, which we may realize to some extent are part of our culture, but we may not be aware that they come from our cultural roots. How do we show our culture to others ? Is it just by our dress, our food preferences, and other obvious habits/behaviors, or are there hidden within values and beliefs that underscore our culture?

The roots of a tree are under the surface—so, too, it is with us. Our central core of beliefs, values, experiences, and cultural heritage are contained within us.

- What part of ourselves do we share with others?
- How do our external actions reflect our inner hidden stories, hidden backgrounds, hidden fears, and hidden insecurities?
- How can appearances be deceiving?
- Can you think of people in your own life who appeared to be one way when in fact they were quite different?

The theme of "Under the Surface" challenges students to think about cultural similarities and differences and to delve into psychological aspects of culture.

A* Invite students to form small groups to consider what "under the surface" might mean. How could they express the idea using other words?

A further discussion of the psychological aspects of "under the surface" should also be encouraged. This will expand students' understanding of surface and may also include references to why some people appear to have an exterior crustiness that is different from their real selves.

The Cultural Base of Our Beliefs

Our underlying beliefs affect what appears on the outside; attitudes are those beliefs that are shown on the surface.

In our schools and society a thin veneer of manners may hide ugly prejudices just under the surface. Where does racism come from?

Conversely, where do tolerance and understanding spring from? What can we as teachers do to encourage them in our classrooms? Surely, providing opportunities for students to walk in the shoes of characters from other cultures is an excellent way to bring home a realization of what it is like to live in them.

A* Since literature offers us the opportunity to experience a multitude of beliefs by reading about those held by characters in books, students should share fiction for young people, such as the following, in which beliefs play important roles.

1. Respect for the beliefs of others

Houston, James. *Frozen Fire*. Two boys, an American and an Inuit, find that skills of both cultures are necessary for their survival when they become lost in the Arctic.

Smucker, Barbara. *Amish Adventure*. A city boy is forced to spend a summer on an Amish farm and makes friends for life.

2. Acceptance of others

Doyle, Brian. *Angel Square*. Tommy finds that in the multicultural mix of Ottawa, people have to be judged as individuals and not by stereotypes.

Doyle, Brian. *Easy Avenue*. Hubbo resists peer pressure at Glebe Collegiate and chooses his own friends.

3. Freedom to express one's self

Spinelli, Jerry. *Maniac McGee*. Maniac's physical talents make him a legend but his fresh responsiveness to all he meets makes him citizen #1.

Spinelli, Jerry. *There's a Girl in My Hammerlock*. Not every girl wants to be a wrestler, but this one determinedly gets her wish.

4. The importance of family

Bell, William. *No Signature*. Wick recovers emotional ground when he discovers his long-errant father.

Little, Jean. *Mama's Going to Buy You a Mockingbird*. Jeremy gives and receives comfort after the death of his father.

Smucker, Barbara. *Jacob's Little Giant*. Looking after a family of giant Canada geese gives Jacob satisfaction and confidence.

Voigt, Cynthia. *Dicey's Song*. Dicey provides great stability for her siblings and her crusty grandmother but she learns a great lesson—you have to let them go.

Emotions Are More Than Skin-Deep

How much in control of our emotions are we as individuals? How much in control are our students? Frequently emotional flare-ups remind us that such strong emotions as love, anger, jealousy, and hate are just under the surface. It should be noted that some emotions such as love can be stifled because of an incorrectly perceived surface expression. This is true in Laurence Yep's *Star Fisher*: Joan's mother has a great deal of love for her daughter but because she cannot do many things due to her lack of English, she has to make Joan do them, thus seeming to be very hard and uncaring.

Readers need to be aware that characters are like volcanoes—eruptions of their inner emotions will eventually explode, and suppression of these only lasts for a period of time. True feelings always surface. We need to realize this to understand the characters.

Joan Lingard's books, such as *The Twelfth Day of July* and *Tug of War*, are set in Belfast, with the leading characters coming from communities of different religious beliefs. Diana Kidd's *Onion Tears* portrays a young Vietnamese refugee in Australia who is unable to share her emotions with the people around her. She is calm on the exterior but turbulent inside. Gudrun Mebs' *Sunday's Child* shares the experience of a young girl in a German orphanage who reveals her true feelings to Ulla, the lady she sees once a week—her Sunday mother. Jim Heneghan's *Promises to Come* sensitively allows the reader to see why a teenage girl who has just arrived in Canada after escaping from Vietnam is so quiet and difficult to communicate with.

Appearances Can Be Deceiving

When we focus on the external appearances of people or cultures we may fail to see and realize the true merits of each. Characters have a right to say, ''I'm not who you think I am!'' This is particularly true when people disguise themselves as something they are not.

Bryan Stevens' biography, *Frank Thompson, Her Civil War Story*, tells of a Union Army soldier who was in fact a woman. Born in Canada as Emma Edwards, she served as a nurse, mail carrier, and spy. In various disguises she ferreted out valuable information behind Confederate lines.

Guardian, in Monica Hughes' *Keeper of the Isis Light*, has changed Olwen so that she is better able to survive on the harsh planet. He also gives her a special outfit, supposedly to protect her from the germs of the settlers—in reality to keep them from seeing the changes he has wrought in her.

The Japanese mother in *So Far from the Bamboo Grove*, by Yoko Kawashima Watkins, has to disguise herself as a Korean soldier.

Animal Culture

Animals and culture? Each year we learn more and more about the intelligence, habits, and group communication of dolphins, wolves, crows, and other animals. A new insight into human culture is sometimes gained by observing animal and insect behavior and ritual. The dance of the honeybee, the changing colors of the salamander reveal much about the nature and society of these creatures. We can ask ourselves, does the changing appearance (surface) of the salamander imply a changing beneath the surface? Does the lizard wear his mask as we do ours? When we see a skunk approaching we tend to move away—not because of what's on the surface, but what lies beneath—the skunk's ability to protect itself by spraying its enemies with foul-smelling liquid. Although not evidenced outwardly, both the beehive and the anthill contain a flurry of activity. Appearances can be deceiving, as in the case of the skunk, beehive, anthill, salamander. So it is with people; our activities and customs can mean one thing while hiding the unexpected beneath.

A* Read aloud Jean Craighead George's *Julie of the Wolves*, a story about a young Inuit girl surviving in the Alaskan tundra with the assistance of a pack of wolves. Pause to record on a chart what knowledge is gained from the book, what is implied and what is questioned by the reader. In addition to this book, students could be reading related titles themselves, keeping track of what they learn about animal culture.

A* Encourage the reading and discussion of the following related titles:

Adams, Richard. *Watership Down*.
George, Jean Craighead. *The Talking Earth*.

George, Jean Craighead. *The Cry of the Crow*.
Malterre, Elona. *The Last Wolf of Ireland*.
Mowat, Farley. *Never Cry Wolf*.
O'Brien, Robert. *Mrs. Frisby and the Rats of NIMH*.

A* To make a bridge between content area reading and fiction, encourage youngsters to explore many genres such as poetry, folklore, and song. Link them thematically by using one animal species, such as a wolf, rabbit, or pig, as the focal point for a cultural exploration.

Walls

Frequently when we are hurting inside we have a tendency to construct a psychological wall around ourselves as a form of protection. Children do this regularly to ward off bullies, to handle teasing or to hide from bad experiences. A good introduction to this concept is to share Carol Fenner's *Randall's Wall*. In it an eleven-year-old boy is shunned by his peers because he is so dirty he stinks. Jean, a socially minded youngster, is determined to bring him out of himself. The scene in which they both jump fully clothed into a bathtub overflowing with soap-bubbles is one of the most hilarious moments in children's literature. The water gradually turns a butterscotch color. Randall's home life is not be to envied, but when his artistic talent is eventually recognized, he is much better able to deal with others. Providing a window into the culture of the poor, the book is also a vehicle for understanding the concept of a person hiding their feelings and culture.

One way to build a wall is to try to become invisible. You are there, but nobody notices you or realizes that you even exist. It is true for the young homeless boy in Eve Bunting's *Fly Away Home*. He and his father, who live in an airport terminal, know that to be different is to be recognized and to be recognized brings trouble. To be invisible is to be safe!

A* Encourage the students to talk about how they could become invisible in their school or community.
    What do they do that makes them become noticed?
    Is it what they wear?
    Can they get into the school without being noticed or seen?
    How? Share strategies that might work.

A* More importantly, ask the students to return and make people notice them. Without making a ruckus, what would they have to do to draw attention to themselves? Speculate on what this tells us about our culture.

Wearing Long Underwear

Many first and second generation immigrant family members feel that underneath they are really still wearing the long underwear of their former culture. This is evidenced by their speech, both in accent and in word selection, as well as by other habits. Although not outwardly ashamed of their old cultural background, they nonetheless do not like it when it unexpectedly shows in ways they had not intended. These "betrayals" might be triggered by photographs, mirrors, fingerprints, aromas, or anything that brings memories of the past.

A* Help children to arrange to visit and interview family members, friends, or neighbors who are recent immigrants. One of the questions they might ask could be: "What cultural behaviors would you like to change now that you are in a new country?"

Many of the students' parents are probably seasoned travellers. How do they feel when they are in other cultural groups? Do they think their cultural underwear is showing? Having the parents share their stories could result in some delightful storytelling sessions.

This concept of cultural discomfort is often noted in literature for young people through the comments or actions of older people, such as parents, grandparents, aunts, or uncles. These individuals do not feel "at home" in their new country. Encourage children to take the place of one of the characters in the following books and relate how they feel—is something embarrassing showing? Laurence Yep's *Child of the Owl, Dragon Wings*, and *Star Fisher*, and Paul Yee's *The Curses of Third Uncle* deal with families newly arrived in the new world.

An exciting change is happening in Canadian schools. Where once many children tried to hide their culture, they are now showing pride in it, using their non-Anglicized names, speaking in their mother tongue, eating traditional food without hesitation. Why? It is partly because there are more children of varying cultures and more effort is being made to recognize and celebrate the multicultural nature of school.

Masks

What better way to hide things under the surface than to wear a mask? A literal definition of a mask is a cover for the body or face, usually for protection or disguise. A figurative definition could be that a mask is something we wear to hide our pleasures, fears, and hurts.

- What happens to a person when he or she puts a mask on?
- Why/how do people wear masks?
- What are some of the types of masks people wear?
- Can masks be considered instruments of power and change?
- Are masks worn to hide or reveal the true identity of the wearer?
- Can wearing a mask have a negative impact? Can masks hide danger?
- How might the donning of a mask make the wearer impervious to censure or criticism?
- Can attitudes become masks?
- How are masks linked to culture?
- Who in a culture is given permission to wear a mask?

A* Challenge students to consider who wears masks in our society. Why? Examples could be divided between professional uses such as those of doctors, police, dentists, etc., and personal ones.

A* Have students read any of the titles below that involve masks. In each case, who wears it? Why? Where does the power of the mask take the characters? *Devil's Arithmetic* by Jane Yolen, *False Face* by Welwyn Wilton Katz, and *Wild Man of the Woods* by Joan Clarke are fascinating explorations of the subject.

Underground Movements

The history of the world is full of groups, often politically motivated, which have sought to change the societies in which they live. These underground movements bring together a diverse assembly of individuals for a specific purpose: to bring peace, to overthrow a ruler, to defeat invaders, or to provide information to outside sources.

During World War II, children and teenagers were often involved in attempts to harass or strongly inconvenience the occupation forces. They were also involved in helping people, particularly the Jews in Europe, to escape to countries which would help them.

Some books which give insight into the involvement of students in underground movements include the following:

Benchley, Nathaniel. *Bright Candles*. Teenage heroes become involved in the Danish underground.

Lowry, Lois. *Number the Stars*. A young Danish girl becomes the key to the successful escape of her Jewish friend's family.

Matas, Carol. *Jesper*. A boy helps the movement by working as a journalist for an underground newspaper while becoming involved in acts of sabotage.

Matas, Carol. *Lisa*. A young Jewish girl follows her brother into the Danish Resistance.

McSwigan, Marie. *Snow Treasure*. A classic story of young Norwegian children hiding their country's gold on their sleds and under their snowmen to help get it out of the country.

Zei, Alki. *Petros' War*. (Translated from the Greek by Edward Fenton.) Acting with the underground, young boys taunt the German soldiers in Athens.

A* Encourage students to read the newspaper and watch TV broadcasts of current conflicts such as that in Bosnia-Herzegovina to see if they can find evidence of an underground movement.

ESCAPE TO FREEDOM

One of the most dramatic movements in North America were the groups of abolitionists and Quakers who operated what was known as safe houses along the Underground Railroad, the route through the Eastern United States along which runaway slaves followed the north star to freedom in Canada. Even today we see evidence of other movements helping people to escape and flee to safety. A good example are those groups trying to help people get into the United States from the Caribbean and Central America. Recent developments have spurred the need for assistance along the route from Hong Kong to Canada and from

Russia to Western Europe.

Books which give insight into this phenomenon are:

Buss, Fran Leeper. *Journey of the Sparrows*, written with the assistance of Daisy Cubias. By the crateload they come—Salvadorean refugees being smuggled into Chicago to struggle to make a living.

Hamilton, Virginia. *The House of Dies Drear*. A mystery associated with an Ohio house's rich history. It was a station on the Underground Railroad.

Heneghan, Jim. *Promises to Come*. One traumatic experience leads to another for a teenage girl who escapes from Vietnam and comes to live with a family in West Vancouver.

Ringgold, Faith. *Aunt Harriet's Underground Railroad in the Sky*. Fantasy and historical fact are integrated in this compelling journey from slavery towards freedom.

Smucker, Barbara. *Underground to Canada*. Two young slave girls flee from the south.

Reflection:
In reading stories of cultural encounters, young people often empathize with well developed characters, their difficulties, and the lessons they learn. Such empathy can provide them with the stimulus to learn more about other cultures as well as their own.

Entre Nous: Cross-Cultural Experiences

We can encourage the awareness of the commonalities exposed beneath the surface to foster an ability to deal with the surface realities of culture when we meet them.

Entre nous—between friends—is relevant to all of us. Most schools have students from many countries, so teachers can encourage opportunities to make friends with individuals from other cultures. What better way to enjoy cross-cultural experiences?

The way we frequently come into contact with another culture is by meeting a person from that cultural group. They may or may not become friends, but they may at least open our eyes to other thoughts, beliefs, and ways of doing things. Our sensitivity to them and to others who appear outwardly different is strengthened by each encounter we have.

Cross-Cultural Friendships

Regardless of age we all know the importance of having good friends. One of the great fears of students is that if they move they will lose their old friends and not have any friends in their new home.
- What brings people together as friends?
  — interests
  — experiences
  — facing a common threat or challenge
  — needs
  — immigration
- What traits do we look for in others?
- What are some initial impediments to friendship?

A* Books which provide young readers with an experience of becoming friends with someone of another culture open the way for international understanding. After students read a selection of the following titles, encourage them to share how some of the characters, and they themselves, become more aware of a new culture.

Bell, William. *Absolutely Invincible*. Four teenagers, each with a disability, form a group and as they go on a motorcycle camping trip become fast friends, each helping the others to accept their challenges.

Ellis, Sarah. *Next-Door Neighbours*. After moving to a new community, twelve-year-old Peggy forms an unusual friendship with a boy who has recently immigrated.

Gavin, Jamila. *Double Dare*. Four short stories about a young boy of East Indian descent in London deal with friendship across cultures, generations, and through time.

Graham, Gail. *Crossfire*. A young American soldier tries to communicate with the enemy—a family of three children.

Houston, James. *Frozen Fire*. Two boys, one Inuit and one white, go out to find a father who has been reported missing. When a storm blows up it takes the skills of both boys to work for their survival and rescue.

Hughes, Monica. *Beyond the Dark River*. An Alberta Hutterite boy looks for help when the children in his commune come down with a strange illness after a disaster has destroyed many cities. He meets another survivor, an Indian girl, and together they go to the remains of the city in search of an answer.

Mowat, Farley. *Lost in the Barrens*. Illustrated by Charles Geer. Two boys, Jamie, a newcomer to the North, and Awasin, a Cree, go on a hunting trip by canoe in the Northwest Territories and become lost. Their survival depends on the sharing of skills from each other's culture.

Smucker, Barbara. *Amish Adventure*. A young boy injured in a car crash goes to stay with an Amish family on their farm. His perception of them changes and he begins to become a friend.

Yep, Laurence. *Star Fisher*. When Joan goes with her family to a small West Virginian town she feels she is an outcast, but by making friends with Bernice, another outcast, she realizes that others will gradually accept her for who she is.

Grandparents

Special bonds of communication and friendship are frequently formed between children and their grandparents. There appears to be something almost magical in the delight of young and old, accepting each other as individuals and sharing mutual pleasures. The old, as guardians of culture, bring out the wisdom in the young and the young bring out the spirit in the old. Both benefit from these friendships, provided that the basis is a mutual sharing of experiences.

A* After reading the following books, students could be encouraged to tell what they value in the friendship between young and old. Find evidence of the culture of the older person and of the child. Later, compare both. Were there differences? How did they manifest themselves?

Bunting, Eve. *The Happy Funeral*. A grandfather's funeral becomes a special event for a Chinese-American family.

Cameron, Ann. *The Most Beautiful Place in the World*. A young Guatemalan boy must move in with his grandmother when his mother remarries and he is not wanted by his stepfather.

Collura, Mary-Ellen Lang. *Winners*. After years spent in foster homes, fifteen-year-old Jordy Threebears returns home to the

Ash Creek Reserve to live with his grandfather.

Doros, Arthur. *Abuela*. A little girl and her Spanish-speaking grandmother have a wonderful adventure in New York City.

Hamilton, Virginia. *Cousins*. Cammy is the only one who has time to visit Granny in the nursing home. They are special friends and it is Granny who comforts her after the death of her cousin.

Härtling, Peter. *Old John*. Translated from the German by Elizabeth D. Crawford. Two children become fond of their 75-year-old grandfather and his idiosyncrasies when he comes to stay with them. After he suffers a stroke they help to care for him, and they miss him terribly when he dies.

MacLachlan, Patricia. *Journey*. Eleven-year-old Journey is left with his grandparents when his mother walks out on him and his sister. Reluctantly he becomes caught up in his grandfather's passion for photography. This eventually helps him to see what he couldn't see with his own eyes—the love that keeps his sense of family alive.

Noumura, Takaaki. *Grandpa's Town*. Translated from the Japanese by Amanda Mayer Stinchecum. A young boy visits his grandfather, now living alone after his wife died, in a small town. The boy delights in meeting his grandfather's friends and visiting favorite places.

Semel, Navaa. *Becoming Gershona*. A young Israeli girl has a special relationship with her new-found American grandfather, who is blind.

Voigt, Cynthia. *Homecoming* and *Dicey's Song*. These are the first two episodes of the Tillerman family saga. When Dicey and her two younger brothers and younger sister are abandoned by their mentally ill mother in a shopping mall parking lot, she decides that they must stay together and find their grandmother.

Yep, Laurence. *Child of the Owl*. A young girl, Casey, goes to live with her grandmother Paw-Paw in San Francisco and in the process learns a lot about her culture.

A* Set up a photography display to trace the growth and maturation of grandparents and grandchildren. These could be actual photos, sketches, photos by the children, or photos clipped from magazines. Annotate any experiences that are captured on film. Often we take photos during culturally based celebrations (weddings, birthdays, educational milestones, etc.). Share these photos in class, as they can be used to define cultural elements.

A* A problem may arise with relationships if grandparents do not speak English and if they try to hold too strongly to their cultural traditions. The young may be turned off and turn away. Encourage the students to find examples of this happening and suggest how communication could be made more positive.

Special Older Friends

Some children, especially those who find themselves in trying, lonely situations, are fortunate to find an unusual person who they instinctively realize can be their friend. To others these old people may seem odd, different, or even crazy, but to the child they are to be trusted and loved, because they treat others with warmth, understanding, and patience. The following books all deal with such friendships.

Cleary, Beverly. *Dear Mr. Henshaw*. A lonely young boy, dealing with his parents' separation and the pressures of elementary school, writes a series of letters to his favorite author.

Donnelly, Elfie. *Offbeat Friends*. When 78-year-old Mrs. Panacek runs away from a mental hospital, her 11-year-old friend Mari knows she must try to help.

Mahy, Margaret. *Memory*. Wandering the streets, teenage Jonny finds a fellow wanderer in old Sophie West. She is suffering from Alzheimer's disease and her only friends seem to be a horde of cats. Taking refuge with her changes his life.

Wallace, Ian. *Chin Chiang and the Dragon's Dance*. When a young boy is afraid to take part in the dragon dance, an elderly woman helps him practice the steps.

The Immigrant Experience

A feature of daily life in North America is the continuing arrival of immigrants from various parts of the world. Some come as business immigrants from such areas as Hong Kong, Taiwan, Japan or Europe: others are refugees from strife-torn areas of Central America, the Kurdish region of Iraq, or what was Yugoslavia.

In anyone's life the move to a new country, especially one with vastly different cultural beliefs and expectations, is an overwhelming experience. To have to cope with a new language, a new system of values for education, a different role for women, "strange" public behavior, and unfamiliar civic responsibility is at times too much for some people. Older immigrants find this process so traumatic that they may just refuse to try to become part of the new society, instead preferring to remain mostly at home. They become literally trapped, depending on their families, especially the children, to look after their needs.

The experience of immigrating to a new country is one which will always be remembered by the children who made the journey, and their children and grandchildren will hear it over and over. Ask if any students or their grandparents or parents have immigrated to North America. The sharing of their stories can be a powerful and moving experience for everyone.

Students should consider the following:
- Why did they leave their homeland?
- What factors influenced their decision?
- Why might they have wanted to stay in their homeland?
- How did they make the arrangements to come?
- How did they travel to North America?

THE LAST DAY

Tomorrow we go! What a time for fears, uncertainties, and doubts. What will tomorrow bring? Will we get there? Questions, questions, questions must go through the minds of people leaving their homes for a new country. Do they have any control over it? Do they have any say as to where they will go?

A* What would it be like to be at the family's last supper in their old homeland? Make this come alive with a role play.

IMMIGRATION TREASURES

Most people who leave their homeland take a treasured possession with them to make links with memories of friends, places, and happy times.

- Whether in a book or in real life, what treasures did people bring with them?
- Can links be made with personal experiences?

- What happened to these treasures in the new land?
- Who valued them?
- Was it a wise decision to bring a particular treasure?
- If you were forced to leave your home and were given only a short time to pack your belongings, what would you take?

PERSONAL MUSEUM

A* We all have things we treasure for one reason or another, and we could use these to make a classroom museum display: "My heritage!" Use photos, objects, newspaper clippings, scrapbooks...

Link the objects with families and individuals in books.

THE ENDLESS DAY

As with any trip, time seems to pass slowly until it is at last the moment to go. Initial fear and anticipation are put aside as we board the plane, train, or ship to take us on our journey.

A* Encourage students to make a frieze of the journey represented in a book, illustrating a segment for each part of it and then taping the individual pictures together.

A* What are the feelings of the characters during the trip? How do they hang on? Devise an emotion graph of the highs and lows of the experience.

Immigration Visions

Before departure	During trip	Arrival	After
Mood			
Expectations			

A* All immigrants have hope, and so regardless how uncomfortable the journey, they tend to believe that everything will be good when they finally arrive. What evidence of this is there in books? A role play would be most effective at this point.

What we see first we remember forever, and we make all our assessments based on it.

A* After the identity of a character is established and the students have followed him or her on their trip, go through the arrival process. What documentation will be needed? Who will they have to be in contact with?

Encourage the students to share their books about immigrant experiences and to share through the eyes and ears of a character their reaction to arriving.

- What did Ellis Island look like? Did the characters feel something when they first saw the Statute of Liberty?
- What did they remember about Montreal or Vancouver when the ship came in or the plane landed?
- How does a prairie city like Edmonton or Regina first look to a person coming from the tropics in winter?

A* In role, elicit responses from the characters about the following:

What was your first feeling upon arrival?

What did you see first?

What was the first smell you noticed?

Was there a more memorable recollection later?

THE FIRST DAYS OF A FIRST YEAR

Once people arrive in their new homelands they often find that it is nothing like what they expected. Those early immigrants hoping to find the streets of America paved with gold and to become wealthy in a short time were in for a rude shock. There was a lot of hard work to do, many misunderstandings to face.

A* Encourage the students, as characters, to tell about these first few days.

- How did they communicate? With whom?
- Were they healthy?
- What were some unexpected sights?
- Did they keep their treasures?
- Did they experience any regrets?
- What were the surprises?
- How did they adapt to change?

A* Frequently it was the children who learned the new language first and thus had to translate for their parents. This would have been most frustrating for a father in a dominant male role. How did he react? Did the child character understand? How did the mother cope?

Immigrants in a New Country

It is important for teachers and students to remember that all people who have immigrated have been caught in a cross-cultural experience. Reading the following books will help students to step into the shoes of characters and be able to share somewhat in the cultural and environmental shock that immigrants may be experiencing today. It is through the process of sharing the thoughts and feelings of characters that the students feel empathy for them and others.

Allma, Ann. *Skateway to Freedom.*

Anderson, Margaret. *The Journey of the Shadow Bairns.*

Arlington, Gabriel. *The Stars Are Upside Down.*

Bell, William. *Absolutely Invincible.*

Harvey, Brett. *Immigrant Girl: Beck of Eldridge Street.* Illustrated by Doborah K. Ray.

Heneghan, Jim. *Promises to Come.*

Hesse, Karen. *Letters from Rifka.*

Horne, Constance. *Nykol and Granny.*

Hurwitz, Johanna. *Once I Was a Plum Tree.*

Kidd, Diana. *Onion Tears.* Illustrated by Lucy Montgomery.

Kraus, Joanna Halpert. *Tall Boy's Journey.* Illustrated by Karen Ritz.

Lord, Bette Bao. *In the Year of the Boar and Jackie Robinson.* Illustrated by Marc Simont.

Lunn, Janet. *Shadow in Hawthorn Bay.*

Namioka, Lensey. *Yang the Youngest and His Terrible Ear.* Illustrated by Kees de Kiefte.

Nixon, Joan Lowry. *Ellis Island, Land of Hope.*

Pearson, Kit. *The Sky Is Falling.*

Smucker, Barbara. *Days of Terror.*

Smucker, Barbara. *Underground to Canada.*

Uchida, Yoshiko. *A Jar of Dreams.*

Whelan, Gloria. *Goodbye Vietnam.*

Yep, Laurence. *The Star Fisher.*

Caught in the Shadow: Cultural Clashes

The word "shadow" can evoke frightening images in the minds of children; evocative images such as eyes gleaming in the dark, long, scary fingers protruding from bushes and trees, bats and witches invade children's imaginations uninvited. Marcia Brown has translated Blaise Cendrar's poem and the resulting book *Shadow* is illustrated with haunting beauty and shadows.

Out of the fire that called forth the many images of shadow, came the ash that was a sacred bond to the life that had gone before. The beliefs and ghosts of the past haunt the present as it stretches into the future. The eerie, shifting image of Shadow appears where there is light and fire and a storyteller to bring it to life.

From their earliest years children are delighted with their own shadows: running with them, running away from them, or just checking over their shoulder to make certain they are following. Dick Gackenbach's *Mr. Wink and His Shadow* captures the delight of shadow-conscious readers. There is no escape from shadows; they follow you around — always!

Shadows in Our Lives

A brainstorming of ideas and words associated with the term "shadow" may reveal a broad range of interpretation by students. Encouraging them to start within themselves, then gradually broaden out to family, school, community, culture, country, and then the world will enrich their responses and provide an increasing degree of abstractness.

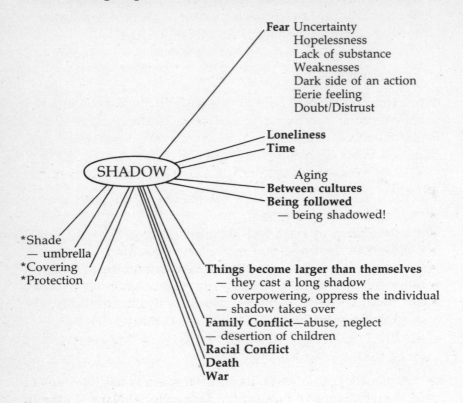

What shadows do we find in our lives? How are they perceived by different cultures? This thematic unit will explore a variety of them, from the impact on individuals (loneliness, being caught between cultures) to the effects of time. Later we will examine the ultimate shadow—war.

CAUGHT IN THE SHADOW OF LONELINESS

Is there any other word but loneliness which can so aptly describe what a shadow feels like to an individual? Individuals of all ages know its power and overwhelming presence. If not checked it can lead to an all-encompassing sense of despair.

This is a commonplace feeling among people who are displaced:

- the loneliness of isolation
- the loneliness of the urban environment
- the loneliness of just moving to a new location
- the loneliness of being an immigrant in a strange land
- the loneliness of being unable to communicate
- the loneliness of being a member of a dysfunctional family
- the loneliness of being a "latchkey" child
- the loneliness within a family, especially if you are breaking away from traditional expectations

A* Encourage students to locate characters who give signs of being lonely. Some of these characters include: Nam-Huong in *Onion Tears* by Diana Kidd, Shabanu in *Shabanu* by Suzanne Fisher Staples, Jacob in *Jacob's Little Giant* by Barbara Smucker.
- What causes their loneliness?
- What do they do to overcome it?
- Do they feel that loneliness is something we all feel?
- How does culture help/hinder this feeling?

A* Students could write to a character to "keep in touch." Which characters in the same or related books might write to the lonely person to buoy up their spirits?

A* Start a pen-pal arrangement with your class and another class. An excellent idea is to have an English as a Second Language class exchange letters with a regular class. If the two groups have a chance to meet, the benefits are doubled.

Does one's culture cast a shadow? Each culture has its own beliefs and customs, which indeed become a kind of shadow. Young immigrant students in a new culture are always aware that the shadow of their old culture hangs over them. Cross-cultural clashes often occur between the old and young because of differing views based on their cultures.

- What happens when a grandparent is of another culture?
- What happens if a grandparent cannot communicate in English?
- How does a child cope with modern life and the traditional "old country" beliefs of grandparents?

The following stories serve to illustrate that within the same culture cross-generational conflicts can easily happen.

Lillian in Paul Yee's *The Curses of Third Uncle* runs into conflict with her mother even as they both struggle to survive in Vancouver's Chinatown. Her father is off raising money for the overthrow of the Manchu Empire and her uncle is threatening to send the women back to China. The same discomfort exists between Casey and her grandmother Paw-Paw in Laurence Yep's *Child of the Owl*. Casey comes to appreciate some of the traditional ways but it is a struggle. In William Bell's *Forbidden City*, the old Communist Chinese leaders, those with the power and control, are being opposed by young students who want freedom.

A classic example is the three youngsters in Lawrence Yep's *Star Fisher*, who, as the first Chinese children in West Virginia, find themselves caught in a triangle of the traditional values of their parents, small-town expectations, and the peer pressure from new friends. A model could be made of this triangle for students to visualize and make comments on.

Manolo, the son of a famous Spanish bullfighter in *Shadow of a Bull* by Maja Wojcieschowska, is expected to follow in his father's footsteps. He must decide on his own, but the cultural pressures are enormous. Only when he faces his first bull does he make up his mind.

A* Encourage students to try to locate novels about conflicts within generations, such as those of two children in a family, one who sticks to the old ways while the other adopts the new ones. This is a perfect scenario for role play.

THE SHADOW OF SLAVERY

Accompanying the publication of more work by African-American writers and illustrators is a desire to share their history, legends, and experiences. Foremost is the continued sharing of the stories of individuals living in the period of slavery in American history. Students need to be encouraged to read such stories to form a composite image of what life was like for slaves on southern plantations.

Some of these are shared in the following titles:

Berry, James. *Ajeemah and His Son.* On the way to claim his bride, a teenage Ghanaian boy and his father are caught by slavers and sold to sugar plantations in Jamaica.

Fox, Paula. *Slave Dancer.* A young boy is kidnapped onto a slave ship to play his flute so that the slaves remain healthy by dancing each day.

Lyons, Mary E. *Letters from a Slave Girl: The Story of Harriet Jacobs.* Based on the letters in her biography, this account tells the trials of a young slave who escapes and hides for many years before fleeing north.

Myers, Walter Dean. *Now Is Your time! The African-American Struggle for Freedom.* A variety of vignettes relating to people and events along the path towards freedom. Highlighted by reproductions of old photographs and documents.

Paulsen, Gary. *Nightjohn.* A cruelly memorable view of slavery as a courageous slave starts to teach a young girl to read, is caught and savagely punished, runs away and yet returns to teach secretly at night.

Smucker, Barbara. *Underground to Canada.* Two young girls follow the hidden signs of the underground railroad to escape north to Canada.

THE SHADOW IN APARTHEID

The changing face of apartheid in South Africa and its gradual demise are the focus of many writers. The following section describes several excellent stories about this difficult subject and offers "Food for Thought," questions that can lead to further discussion and reflection. The situation in South Africa has rapidly changed so dramatically that many of the novels available offer more of a reflection on the struggle to overcome previous situations than a glimpse of the current situation.

A* Encourage students to assemble a South Africa wall covered with newspaper and magazine clippings relating to the current situation. One section could also contain references to previous developments in the path to the development of a new country.

Love, David
Dianne Case

Anna Jantjies and her family are "colored"—descendants of white settlers and black slaves or indigenous people in the days before interracial relationships became illegal in South Africa. Anna cares for her baby sister in their shanty on Cape Flats while her mother works as a housekeeper for a wealthy white family in Cape Town. Her father has a drinking problem and cannot keep a steady job. There is tension between Anna's father and her older half-brother, David, whom she idolizes. Anna relates the happy and sad times with David, who becomes involved in illegal activities to escape the poverty of his home life.

The author based this story on her mother's own childhood and wrote it "...to make people aware of a very real section of the South African community" and "to share a culture with those who do not know about it." She accomplishes this very successfully. The shocking living conditions of the family are clearly portrayed, yet Anna retains a sense of hope for the future.

A* When David is jailed at the end of the story, he leaves Anna a box containing all he owns. Though there is nothing in the pathetic collection of broken blades, a few cents, bits of screws or scraps of string that Anna can use, she cannot throw the box away. What do these objects represent to Anna? If Anna could send a box to David, what objects might she include as symbols of her life?

- How does the apartheid system affect black South African families?
- How does a family cope with enforced separation from loved ones?
- What keeps a family going despite threats from without (society) and from within (internal family problems)?
- What is the role of education in changing society?

Waiting for the Rain
Sheila Gordon

This powerful story chronicles nine years in the lives of two South African youths. Tengo is a black "boy" on the farm owned by Frikkie's white uncle and the two children play together when Frikkie stays at the farm during school vacations. Frikkie is an indifferent student who longs for the day when he will inherit the farm; Tengo dreams of a college education. The changing times in South Africa pull them in opposite directions and threaten their future plans. Finally, as soldier and student, they are forced to confront one another and to make choices that will alter both their lives.

FOOD FOR THOUGHT

- What are the signs of change in this society?
- How do people react to the inevitability of change?
- What happens to the bonds of friendship in a society that discriminates on the basis of race?
- What role does education play in shaping social change?
- As key players in resistance movements, what pressures are felt by young black students?

Journey to Jo'burg
Chain of Fire

Beverley Naidoo

In *Journey to Jo'burg* a thirteen-year-old village girl, Naledi, is forced by a family emergency to travel to Johannesburg, where her mother is employed as a housekeeper for a wealthy white family. It is here that Naledi first learns about the struggles of her people in Soweto and experiences first-hand the inequities between blacks and whites in South Africa.

In the sequel, *Chain of Fire*, Naledi, at the age of fifteen, helps to organize a peaceful student protest against the government's plan to evict the people of her village and resettle them in a barren "homeland." An attack on the demonstrators by armed police is the first of several acts of violence sanctioned by the government. The book relates how villagers work together, despite tragedy, becoming human links in a "chain of fire" dedicated to social change.

FOOD FOR THOUGHT

- What is the role young people played in the resistance movement in South Africa?
- How did these people cope with cultural change in their society?
- How does an individual summon up the courage to take a difficult stand in times of turmoil?
- What is the price of resistance (physical, emotional, social, etc.)? The consequences for society as a whole?

Paper Bird

Maretha Maartens
Translated by Madeleine van Biljon

Adam is a young boy who lives in the township of Phameng, outside the city of Bloemfontein. He supports his widowed mother and younger siblings by selling newspapers in the city. When mob violence erupts on the road between the township and the city, Adam must decide whether he will continue to work, risking the safety of himself and his family by so doing. Yet he is desperate for the few rand he requires to feed the family.

FOOD FOR THOUGHT

- What fears do young black South Africans face?
- How do they deal with these fears?
- How do these young people retain a sense of hope for the future? (A newspaper bird, for instance, with its power of flight, becomes Adam's symbol of hope.)

At the Crossroads
Over the Green Hills
Rachel Isadora

In a typical South African township a group of children feel great excitement as they wait at the crossroads to greet their fathers, who have been away for ten months working in the mines. After an all-night vigil, the joyful reunion takes place.

A young boy in the second book helps his mother as he ties a bag of mussels on their goat so that they can walk across many miles of the Transkei countryside to visit his grandmother.

FOOD FOR THOUGHT

- How do families cope with enforced separation from loved ones?
- How do individuals in a community support one another in times of trial?
- How do family bonds keep love, happiness, and hope alive?

Caught in the Shadow of Death

The ultimate shadow is that of death. It is not a subject that many adults and students are comfortable discussing. Indeed, in western society it is often deemed not suitable for students, yet they generally do not have any trouble with it. Students deserve the right to read about death in children's literature before they are unexpectedly forced to deal with it in their own lives.

Some good books for young people focus on death in a way that honestly expresses the full range of emotions associated with the loss felt by the individuals involved. Quality writers often have a positive attitude and share ways in which characters cope with the experience. As readers we can be empowered by our reading experience.

A* Students could have a profitable discussion sharing the feelings of characters in the following books.

When a pet dies how do you react? A young boy in Judith Viorst's *The Tenth Good Thing about Barney* comes up with a list of ten things that made his cat special.

When a father dies, as in Jean Little's *Mama's Going to Buy You a Mockingbird*, it is very difficult for the children, but Jeremy is able to have some time with his father at the end. This book raises a good discussion point—when do young people want to be told if something serious is going to happen? Do they really want to be protected?

When it is your baby sister who dies, as in Sarah Ellis' *The Baby Project*, the shock reverberates for a long time.

When a friend dies, as in Katherine Paterson's *Bridge to Terabitha*, or as in Doris Smith's *A Taste of Blackberries*, or your sister as in Jean Fritz's *Homesick*, the shock, hurt, sorrow, and grief can be almost unbearable.

When it is you who are going to die, the questions are even more difficult. Mike, suffering from leukemia in Monica Hughes' *Hunter in the Dark*, is determined to do one last thing—to shoot a stag.

What kind of control do you have over your life when disease strikes?

The power of belief is illustrated in Eleanor Coerr's *Sadako and the Thousand Paper Cranes*, in which a girl believes that if she just made 1,000 paper-folded cranes she would get better.

The death of grandparents is often told in a no-nonsense manner. They may have died, but youngsters can remember them through special possessions of theirs. Children accept this passing, reflect sadly, but also recall happy times. This response can be seen in Dayal Kaur Khalsa's *Tales of a Gambling Grandma* and Sheryl McFarlane's *Waiting for the Whales*.

Witnessing an old culture dying is unusual in literature for young people, but Kevin Major in *Blood Red Ochre* shares a backward glimpse at the last of the Beothuk tribe in Newfoundland.

There is no more powerful message about being caught in the shadow of death than in the picture book, *My Hiroshima*, by Junko Morimoto. A little Japanese girl narrates what her experiences were like before, during, and after the fall of the atomic bomb.

Reflection:

The value of good books for young people is that they allow readers to experience life while offering them the security of a certain distance from a reality that might be too frightening or sorrow-filled for them at a given time.

Are we ever ready for the death of a loved one?
How do different cultures deal with death?
How do different cultures remember their dead?
Can you see evidence of old cultures dying?

Caught in the Shadow of War

Good novels about war give readers the experience of being right there, of sensing the agony of both participants and helpless bystanders. The characters are real people, fully developed, thinking, feeling individuals.

The shadow of war is a powerful metaphor that adds to the reading and sharing of war novels. Young people do not have a say in the starting of the world's wars, yet their lives are inextricably affected by them. It is important for teachers to remind students that the shadow of war is cast on both sides of the front lines. Thus, it is imperative that novels, particularly those in translation, by such writers as Hans Peter Richter, Roberto Innocenti, and Sook Nyul Choi, be included.

The impact of war in the '90s is immediate. Highlighted by the dramatic coverage by CNN and other major American television networks, Operation Desert Storm was viewed in millions of homes all over the world as it happened. What was the effect on student viewers? Were they made more sensitive to the plight of the innocent bystanders caught in the crossfire? The tragedy is that such coverage may make students less sensitive, more accepting of killing and senseless acts of violence without any emotional second thoughts. Thus the need for exposure to good novels that lead to a reflective response.

The following figure illustrates situations in which children find themselves during wartime, and which are reflected in novels being written for young people. In wartime the best and worst aspects of fighting cultures often reveal themselves. This figure can be a starting point for discussions about war and its effects on children as well as others.

THE SHADOW OF WAR

The Child

CAUGHT	FEELINGS
Being in the wrong place	Uncertainty
Life changes dramatically	Guilt
Changing friendships	

DEATH	
Family members	Disbelief
Friends	Sorrow
Being alone	Anger
	Rage

ESCAPE	
Flee	Fear
Refugees	Betrayal
In hiding	

SURVIVAL	
Lack of shelter	
Lack of clothing	Cold
Lack of food	Hunger

RESISTANCE	Determination
	Commitment

Teachers can involve students and evoke insightful responses by reading aloud one of the war novels listed later in this section. It is important to select a novel which offers a sensitive look at the life of a youngster, sharing the culture of the times and giving an honest account of the changes brought about as the war progresses.

The oral sharing of an outstanding novel is a gift that we can give to students that will be remembered for a lifetime. When the oral interpretation is planned and effectively presented, the power of the writer evokes immediate images within the listeners as they participate in the plot. As teachers we should provide pauses for reflection, for mutual discussion, for dreaming and recall.

An example of an outstanding book which raises many cultural issues is *Number the Stars* by Lois Lowry. Set in Copenhagen during the German occupation, this book tells of Ellen and Annemarie, who accept the presence of German soldiers until they start to round up the Jews. Ellen's family is Jewish. This Newbery Award-winning novel demonstrates how ordinary people undertake acts of personal bravery and integrity to stand up for what they believe in. Annemarie's family are involved in assisting Jewish people to escape by hiding them in the bottom of fishing boats. They "adopt" Ellen and even manage to convince soldiers searching their apartment that she is their daughter.

The book itself is an excellent read-aloud. Lowry is a skilled writer with a good visual sense who creates a tension that will appeal to all listeners.

A* As you read this novel aloud, encourage students to read other war novels and compare and contrast them with Lowry's book. What examples of different cultures do we witness through the novels? Have the students find other examples of cross-cultural conflict. Two appropriate examples in this case are Hans Peter Richter's *Friedrich* and Doris Orgel's *The Devil in Vienna*, both of which examine the concept of changing friendship in wartime.

Novel Blitz!

An appropriate way to start or continue this theme, due to the large number of resources available (see the bibliography), is to blitz the classroom with war novels. Booktalks by the teacher or teacher-librarian will serve as a motivational invasion. Children are in cultural conflict in all of these books, and all of them are in the shadow of war. Although innocent bystanders, their lives will never be the same again.

A. World War II Novels

Signs of the war coming are to be found in only a limited number of books.

Kay, Maria. *Storm Warning.*

Kerr, Judith. *When Hitler Stoke Pink Rabbit.*

Little, Jean. *From Anna.*

Richter, Hans Peter. *Friedrich.*

Children in these books are caught right in the middle of the action.

Bishop, Claire. *Twenty and Ten.*

Frank, Anne. *The Diary of a Young Girl.*

Gallaz, Christophe, and Roberto Innocenti. *Rose Blanche.*

Hartman, Evert. *War without Friends.*

Orlev, Uri. *The Island on Bird Street.*

Orlev, Uri. *Man from the Other Side.*

Reiss, Johanna. *The Upstairs Room.*

Ter Haar, Jaap. *Boris.*

Wayne, Kyra Petrovksaya. *Shurik: A Story of the Siege of Leningrad.*

In Britain young people are actively taking part in the war effort.

Bawden, Nina. *Carrie's War.*

Cooper, Susan. *Dawn of Fear.*

Walsh, Jill Paton. *Fireweed.*

Westall, Robert. *The Machine Gunners.*

Young people in Germany are affected by the war too.

Nöstlinger, Christine. *Fly Away Home.* Translated by Anthea Bell.

Orgel, Doris. *The Devil in Vienna.*

Richter, Hans Peter. *Friedrich.* Translated by Edite Kroll.

Richter, Hans Peter. *The Time of the Young Soldiers.* Translated by Anthea Bell.

Novels of resistance are very popular with readers as they give a sense of being actively involved in the campaign to defeat the enemy.

Benchley, Nathaniel. *Bright Candles.*

Lowry, Lois. *Number the Stars.*

Matas, Carol. *Jesper.*

Matas, Carol. *Lisa.*

Morpurgo, Michael. *Waiting for Anya.*
Wuorio, Eva-Lis. *Code: Polonaise.*
Zei, Alki. *Petros' War.*

It is time to flee!
Kasper, Vancy. *Escape to Freedom.*
Kerr, Judith. *When Hitler Stole Pink Rabbit.*
Pearson, Kit. *The Sky Is Falling.*

The war affects Japanese youngsters as well.
Maruki, Toshi. *Hiroshima No Pika.*
Morimoto, Junko. *My Hiroshima.*
Say, Allen. *The Bicycle Man.*
Watkins, Yoko Kawashima. *So Far from the Bamboo Grove.*

What happens on the West Coast of North America after the bombing of Pearl Harbor?
Garrigue, Sheila. *The Eternal Spring of Mr. Ito.*
Kogawa, Joy. *Naomi's Road.*
Uchida, Yoshiko. *Journey to Topaz.*

Thousands of miles away from the warfront the lives of youngsters are affected by the war effort.
Greene, Bette. *Summer of My German Soldier.*
Hahn, Mary. *Stepping on the Cracks.*

B. Asian War Novels

Korea
Choi, Sook Nyul. *Year of the Impossible Goodbyes.*
Watkins, Yoko Kawashima. *So Far from the Bamboo Grove.*

Vietnam
Bunting, Eve. *The Wall.*
Southeast Asia
Ho, Minfong. *The Clay Marble.*

C. African War Novels
Watson, James. *No Surrender.*

The Rising Phoenix: Cultural Reawakenings

The phoenix, a mythical bird of great beauty, was believed to have lived for 500 to 600 years in the Arabian wilderness before burning itself on a pyre and rising from the ashes with the freshness of youth. It is still considered an emblem of immortality.

Today a phoenix represents a person or creature that has been renewed or restored. It is often taken as the symbol of rebirth, rising as it does from the ashes.

Recently, there has been an unusual proliferation of books and magazines articles about the Mayas. Why has this happened? Celebrations of Columbus's arrival in 1492 have inspired interest in the area and a closer look at the culture of the times, but there is something else that intrigues the researchers and writers, something else that exudes the power of Mayan beliefs.

The descendants of the Mayas in Central America are experiencing persecution and many are fleeing the area. What is exciting is that they are taking stories with them. When they arrive in Canada or the United States they do not come empty handed—their sense of story helps them with their own cultural identity.

The reawakening of interest in Mayan culture is but one example of a worldwide resurgence of nationalistic, cultural feelings among ethnically diverse peoples. Although the majority of available books in English about other cultures have been written by non-natives, a remarkable development is occurring in that cultures are now being written about by members of them.

A characteristic of the 1990s is a dramatic rise in the general interest in the culture of aboriginal peoples throughout the world. They in turn are trying to preserve their cultures before they are assimilated by other countries. As modern national states and continents try to unify there appears to be a very strong backlash of local cultural preservation. In this section we shall examine the reawakenings of the cultures of many groups—first with the Mayas themselves, then other aboriginal peoples.

Cultural Reawakenings: The Mayas

Long before the arrival of Columbus, the Mayas had the major civilization on the Yucatan Peninsula. They lived in what are parts of present-day Mexico, Belize, Guatemala, Honduras, and El Salvador. They were at their height between 200 AD and 900 AD. Advanced in so many ways, particularly the arts and architecture, they are frequently compared to the Ancient Greeks.

When Paris was but a village the Mayas were carving magnificent palaces out of the jungle and playing a ball game for life or death. The ball was seen as a symbol for the movement of the sun. It was part of the Mayan love of ritual. At the centre were the gods, the source of all life, yet it was the king who intervened with them—hence, the elaborate temples and palaces.

One of the greatest achievements was the Mayan calendar, based on astronomical observations. This allowed the Mayas to understand and measure time, and even predict some astrological events such as solar eclipses. Their number system was more advanced than the Roman or Greek ones, for they had developed the concept of zero.

The collapse of Mayan civilization remains unexplained. Modern archeologists speculate that the abrupt abandonment of cities such as Tikal, Palenque, Copán, and Chichén Itzá may have been due to overpopulation, war, destructive farming practices, or extreme social divisions between rich and poor.

Recent television programs have shown Guatemalan Mayan refugees in Mexico rebuilding the ruins of Edzna. In the process they are finding out about themselves and their culture. They have discovered a treasure inside themselves: knowledge of their culture.

A* The ruins are viewed as part of the heritage of all humanity, being created by artists on the same level as daVinci, but even though they were anonymous they had marvelous techniques. Encourage students to find art books with photographs of the work of Mayan artists, or try to create a work of art in the Mayan style.

A* Today the Mayas are under siege. They have been caught in the civil war in Guatemala. So far more than 100,000 have been killed and 40,000 have disappeared. Yet they endure. Ask students to find newspaper and magazine clippings about the plight of the Mayas.

A* Students will be fascinated by viewing a series of videos, *The Voyage of the Mimi II*, produced by the Bank Street College of Education. Each of the ten videos in the series has a fifteen-minute segment with actors in role enacting a historical event. This is followed by a fifteen-minute segment in which the actors come out of role to explain the concepts and facts associated with the event. One segment features a modern Mayan girl. Focused on archeology, math, and science, the package consists of videos, student textbooks, and computer software.

A* Encourage students to locate Mayan legends and tales to give examples of their culture. Two excellent examples:

Shetterly, Susan Hand. *The Dwarf-Wizard of Uxmal*. Illustrated by Robert Shetterly. A boy hatched from an egg has magical powers and in one night builds a temple.

Wisniewski, David. *Rain Player*. Outstanding cut-paper illustrations accompany the story of young Pik, who takes the fate of his drought-stricken people on himself when he challenges the rain god Chac to a ball game.

A* Focusing on the Mayas encourages an integration of interest in various subject areas. Social studies, science, and mathematics all intertwine in this topic. Some titles of interest include the following.

Baudez, Claude, and Sydney Picasso. *Lost Cities of the Maya.*
Beck, Barbara L. *The Ancient Maya.*
Carver, Norman. *Silent Cities and Mexico and the Maya.*
Coe, Michael. *Breaking the Maya Code.*
Coe, Michael. *The Maya.*
Dworking, Mark J. *The Riddles and Rediscovery of a Lost Civilization: Maya.*
Greene, Jacqueline Dembar. *The Maya.*
Leonard, Jonathan Norton. *Ancient America.*
McKissack, Patricia. *The Maya.*
Meyer, Carolyn, and Charles Gallenkamp. *The Mystery of the Ancient Maya.*
Odijk, Pamela. *The Mayas.*
Schele, Linda, and David Freidel. *A Forest of Kings: The Untold Story of the Ancient Maya.*
Wright, Ronald. *Time among the Maya.*

Cultural Reawakenings: The Aboriginal Peoples of Australia

Legends and tales from the outback of Australia have long fascinated young readers. The drama of unique characters and places is enhanced by the vivid illustrations in some picture book versions.

Australian publishers encourage the publication of aboriginal writers. *Uncle Willie Mackenzie's Legends of the Goundirs* was told by Sylvia Cairns and illustrated by Fred Cobbo. Dick Roughsey was noted as being one of the foremost of the aboriginal artists. Many others have since written or illustrated tales for children.

A* Encourage students to locate these books and reflect on the major themes in them.

Abdula, Ian. *As I Grew Older: The Life and Times of a Nunga Growing Up along the River Murray.*
Coe, Mary. *Windradyne—A Wiradjurl Koori.* Illustrated by Isabel Coe.
Djugurba. *Tales from the Spirit Time.*

Lofts, Pamela. *The Bat and the Crocodile*. Illustrated by children in the Warmun aboriginal community at Turkey Creek.

Lofts, Pamela. *Echidna and the Shade Tree*. Illustrated by aboriginal children.

Lofts, Pamela. *How the Birds Got Their Colours*. Illustrated by aboriginal children.

Lofts, Pamela. *The Kangaroo and the Porpoise*. Illustrated by children in the Belyuen aboriginal community near Darwin.

Lofts, Pamela. *Warnayarra: The Rainbow Snake*. Illustrated by the children in the Lajamanu aboriginal community on the edges of the Tyanami Desert.

Lofts, Pamela. *When the Snake Bites the Sun*. Illustrated by aboriginal children.

McRobbie, Narelle. *Bip, the Snapping Kangaroo*. Illustrated by Grace Fielding.

Meeks, Arone Raymond. *Enora and the Black Crane*.

Narritjan, Maymuru. *The Milky Way*.

O'Brien, May L. *The Legend of the Seven Sisters: A Traditional Aboriginal Story from Western Australia*. Illustrated by Sue Wyatt.

Roughsey, Dick. *The Giant Devil Dingo*.

Roughsey, Dick. *The Rainbow Serpent*.

Solomon, Selena. *Dabu the Baby Dugong*. Illustrated by Dennis Nona.

Utemorrah, Daisy. *Do Not Go Around the Edges*. Illustrated by Pat Torres.

Cultural Reawakenings: First Nations

In recent years North America has seen a resurgence of cultural awareness among the peoples of the First Nations. This is the final step in a three-pronged development. Initially their legends and stories were part of their oral heritage and were written down by trained observers, such as anthropologist Franz Boas and others, committed to capturing the authentic spirit of the stories. Members of the community were consulted about details. Later, writers simply read the accounts of early anthropologists and retold the stories, sadly sometimes without feeling for their authenticity. Today many First Nations writers are telling their own stories. This exciting development is the source of much interest and pride.

A* Students should be encouraged to read the following titles, listening for the special voice of the teller, not expecting the plot line to follow the tradition of other cultures.

FOLKTALES

Cohlene, Terri (adaptor). *Clamshell Boy: A Makah Legend.* Illustrated by Charles Reasoner.

Okanagan Tribal Council. *How Food Was Given.*

Okanagan Tribal Council. *How Names Were Given.*

Okanagan Tribal Council. *How Turtle Set the Animals Free.*

Rossetti, Bernadette (translator & reteller). *Musdzi 'Udada/The Owl.*

Scribe, Murdo. *Murdo's Story: A Legend from Northern Manitoba.* Illustrated by Terry Gallagher.

Taylor, C.J. *The Ghost and the Lone Warrior.*

Taylor, C.J. *How Two-Feather Was Saved from Loneliness.*

Taylor, C.J. *Little Water and the Gift of the Animals.*

PICTURE BOOKS

Armstrong, Jeannette. *Neekna and Chemai.*

Bear, Glecia. *Two Little Girls Lost in the Bush: A Cree Story for Children.* Edited and translated by Freda Ahenakew and H.C. Wolfart. Illustrated by Jerry Whitehead.

Gayle, Donald. *Sooshewan: Child of the Beothuk.* Illustrated by Shawn Steffler.

King, Thomas. *A Coyote Columbus Story.* Pictures by William Kent Monkman.

Kusugak, Michael Arvaarluk. *Baseball Bats for Christmas.* Art by Vladyana Krykorka.

Kusugak, Michael Arvaarluk. *Hide and Sneak.* Art by Vladyana Krykorka.

Munsch, Robert, and Michael Kusugak. *A Promise Is a Promise.* Illustrated by Vladyana Krykorka.

Wheeler, Bernelda. *A Friend Called "Chum".* Illustrated by Andy Stout.

Wheeler, Bernelda. *I Can't Have Bannock, but the Beaver Has a Dam.* Illustrated by Herman Bekkering.

Wheeler, Bernelda. *Where Did You Get Your Moccasins?* Illustrated by Herman Bekkering.

FICTION

Sterling, Shirley. *My Name Is Seepeetza.*

YOUNG ADULT

Culleton, Beatrice. *April Raintree.*

POETRY

Bouchard, Dave. *The Elders Are Watching.* Illustrated by Roy Henry Vickers.
George, Chief Dan. *My Heart Soars.*

Cultural Reawakenings: African-Americans

There has been an exciting renaissance of literature within the African-American community in the United States. As the establishment and continuation of the Coretta Scott King Award indicates, more and more quality books are being published than ever before.

A* Encourage students to read the following titles, noting as they do the universal themes that affect all of us.

PICTURE BOOKS

Adoff, Arnold. *Black Is Brown Is Tan.*
Bryan, Ashley. *All Night, All Day: A Child's First Book of African-American Spirituals.*
Bryan, Ashley. *The Cat's Purr.*
Clifton, Lucille. *The Boy Who Didn't Believe in Spring.* Illustrated by Brinton Turkle.
Clifton, Lucille. *Everett Anderson's Goodbye.* Illustrated by Ann Grifalconi.
Clifton, Lucille. *Everett Anderson's Nine Month Long.* Illustrated by Ann Grifalconi.
Flournoy, Valerie. *The Patchwork Quilt.* Illustrated by Jerry Pinkney.
Hale, Sarah Josepha. *Mary Had a Little Lamb.* Photographs by Bruce McMillan.
McKissack, Patricia. *Flossie and the Fox.* Illustrated by Rachel Isadora.

McKissack, Patricia. *Mirandy and Brother Wind*. Illustrated by Jerry Pinkney.

Pinkney, Gloria Jean. *Back Home*. Illustrated by Jerry Pinkney.

Steptoe, John. *Stevie*.

Walter, Mildred Pitts. *Brother to the Wind*. Illustrated by Leo and Diane Dillon.

FICTION

Collier, James, and Christopher Collier. *Jump Ship to Freedom*.

Greenfield, Eloise. *Daydreamers*. Illustrated by Tom Feelings.

Greenfield, Eloise. *Talk about a Family*.

Guy, Rosa. *The Friends*.

Hamilton, Virginia. *The House of Dies Drear*. Illustrated by Eros Keith.

Hamilton, Virginia. *M.C. Higgins the Great*.

Hamilton, Virginia. *The Mystery of Drear House*.

Hamilton, Virginia. *Zeely*. Illustrated by Symeon Shimin.

Lester, Julius. *Long Journey Home*.

Lester, Julius. *To Be a Slave*. Illustrated by Tom Feelings.

Myers, Walter Dean. *Fallen Angels*.

Myers, Walter Dean. *Fast Sam, Cool Clyde & Stuff*.

Myers, Walter Dean. *The Outside Shot*.

Myers, Walter Dean. *Scorpions*.

Myers, Walter Dean. *Won't Know Until I Get There*.

Taylor, Mildred. *The Gold Cadillac*. Illustrated by Michael Hays.

Taylor, Mildred. *Roll of Thunder, Hear My Cry*.

Thomas, Joyce C. *The Golden Pasture*.

Thomas, Joyce C. *Journey*.

Thomas, Joyce C. *Marked by Fire*.

Walter, Mildred Pitts. *Justin and the Best Biscuits in the World*. Illustrated by Catherine Stock.

Cultural Reawakenings: Hey, I'm ME!

An exciting aspect of this theme is the number of books which reflect the gradual cultural awakening of individuals. They have not been aware of their past, nor cared to be, but something changes in them and they share their cultural discoveries with openness and growing pride.

A* Ask students how aware they are of their own cultures. When did they begin to take pride in them? If they do not, discuss how they could get information about them.

A* Compare the reactions of students to uncovering their culture with the characters in the following books.

Collura, Mary-Ellen Lang. *Winners.* After years of resentment toward the "white" culture have left him feeling alienated and angry, fifteen-year-old Jordy Threebears' life changes dramatically when he goes to stay with Joe Speckledhawk, his maternal grandfather. Through a gift of a wild mare, an understanding teacher, and a blind girl, Jordy gradually gains confidence in himself and takes pride in his cultural heritage.

Houston, James. *Drifting Snow: An Arctic Search.* Twelve-year-old Apoutee's identity papers were lost when she was flown out to a hospital in the south to be treated for her tuberculosis. Now, as Elizabeth Queen, she returns to the Arctic in search of her family, her culture, and her language.

Hughes, Monica. *My Name Is Paula Popowich.* Eleven-year-old Paula Herman leaves Toronto with her mother to live in Edmonton, where her mother grew up. As she adjusts to the move she uncovers some of her family roots, including the truth about her father's death and the strained relationship with her grandparents. She finds a remarkable sense of belonging as she explores her Ukrainian heritage.

Paulsen, Gary. *Dogsong.* Russell Suskitt, a young inuit boy, feels he does not know his own culture, so he goes to old Oogruk and learns about the power of old songs and the strategies for surviving. Running a dog team over the icy terrain brings him to a hard-fought awareness of the validity of the old ways.

These stories are not the only ones available. Students will find others as they read their way through many of the titles suggested in this book.

Reflection:

Any period of reawakening is a time of excitement, rebirth, new beginnings, and rejoicing. This is precisely the case with the quartet of cultural groups mentioned in this theme.

- What is the importance of story to culture?
- How do cultures assimilate other cultures?
- Why is there a resurgence of interest in the literature and myths of cultural groups?

Chapter 4

Exploring the Cultural Literary Experience

Cultural Voices

Voices from many cultures are being heard as never before as an increasing number of distinguished writers create books which offer a unique cultural experience for readers. Many write about other cultures, some are voices from within cultural groups, yet through their sensitive portrayal of individuals and events, they all offer valuable insights. They have the power to increase the awareness of students about the lives of others and, it is hoped, to give them just a bit more tolerance and respect for others.

Teachers who are themselves active readers will recognize that the unique character of each book will suggest novel ways to share it with students so that it becomes a memorable experience in their lives. Teachers and librarians make books accessible to students by reading them aloud well. Thus, time must be spent on the oral interpretation of each title to enhance the effect the author is trying to achieve.

An exciting aspect of working on this book was the inclusion of ideas and strategies that several practicing teachers have found to be stimulating, thought-provoking, and valid for their intermediate students. The same format is used for approaching all the novels listed here. After a story synopsis, several questions are posed in the "Food for Thought" section. These are designed to reflect our thoughts about the major issues dealt with in each book and directions you may take in exploring them. If you find it difficult to deal with the questions, skip over them and return to them afterwards as a reflective activity. All activities are designed to be as open-ended as possible, thus allowing for creative expression in your classroom. Part of the excitement of these novels is that there are so many directions you can go in with them. Obviously, you as the teacher will have to select ones that are most appropriate for your students at the moment.

Many of the suggested activities include having students find relevant quotes from novels. This is done to highlight the power of each novel, both in terms of the impact of the ideas and of the writing style. I have recently found that a bulletin board display of quotes from books is one of the most effective ways to make students aware of good writing. It gets them to say, "I wish I had written that!"

The following titles are included in the Key Book lists because they offer students a worthwhile cultural experience. They are recommended for excellence in writing and realistic portrayal of a culture. Folktales have been dealt with in an earlier chapter, as has historical fiction, itself so valuable in helping place modern cultural expression in perspective. Recommended translated works of literature for young people are included later in this chapter.

No book has a "right" age level; rather it depends on the individual student, and so I trust that you will take suggestions about age levels as approximate indications of where I have found these books to be valuable.

It is important to share a number of novels in a variety of ways, rather than to have just one title accompanied by a myriad of generic activities. Build on the activities mentioned here; make them your own.

Key Books

9+	Onion Tears
	The Most Beautiful Place in the World
	Tikta'liktak
10+	Number the Stars
	A Jar of Dreams
	Underground to Canada
11+	Kiss the Dust
	Star Fisher
	The Curses of Third Uncle
	The Eternal Spring of Mr. Ito
	Homesick: My Own Story

Key Books 9+

Onion Tears
Diana Kidd

THE STORY

A young Vietnamese refugee has been taken in by a woman, also of Vietnamese descent, who runs a restaurant. This young woman has a past so nightmarish for her that she is unable to speak, leading her schoolmates to think she is dumb. Even though Nam-Huong works in "Auntie's" restaurant with the cook Chu Minh, she leads a lonely life and to survive she writes letters home to her friends the yellow canary, the white duck, and the water buffalo to inquire about her family. Gradually, she is able to break out of her protective cocoon and become part of life around her.

This is a simply written tale with a powerful impact due to strong characterizations and sensitivity to feelings.

FOOD FOR THOUGHT

- What are things that bring tears to your eyes?
- What are the different kinds of tears?
- What are real tears?
- What are onion tears?
- Shedding tears—is it good for you?

"WHY CAN'T I CRY REAL TEARS?"

Nam-Huong asks this question in all honesty. Are there other situations in which students may find themselves in which they would feel the same way?
- Why are tears so important?
- When do we cry?

- Who cries?

Encouragement may bring out such unexpected answers as the following:
- Crying is important when somebody dies.
- Tears are part of the grieving process.
- We just don't want to let go of the past.
- As we cry we help rid ourselves of the ghosts of the past.

A* Students will be concerned about Nam-Huong's inability to talk. They will want to talk about this lack of talk! Why? She can't, she's shy, she's dumb, she doesn't know English or... The students should also reflect on the fact that because she doesn't speak she has to endure ridicule, hostility, loneliness, and increased cultural/environmental shock.

LETTERS OF TEARS

The book contains many letters which Nam-Huong writes to her best friend, the canary, as well as to the water buffalo and white duck.

A* Encourage the students to examine these letters to see what changes in them they can detect.

Letter	Tone	Observations (Facts Given)	Reader Insight
#1			
#2			
#3			
#4			

The insights gained by a close reading of these letters for what they really say will be very much like peeling away the various layers of an onion. They are actually a means for Nam-Huong to uncover and admit to the horrors that have happened to her family. She has no frame of reference to explain past stories, and to some extent they are the voice of her subconscious.

A* After reading the first letter, have the students make a visual representation, within an onion tear, of the feelings of Nam-Huong.

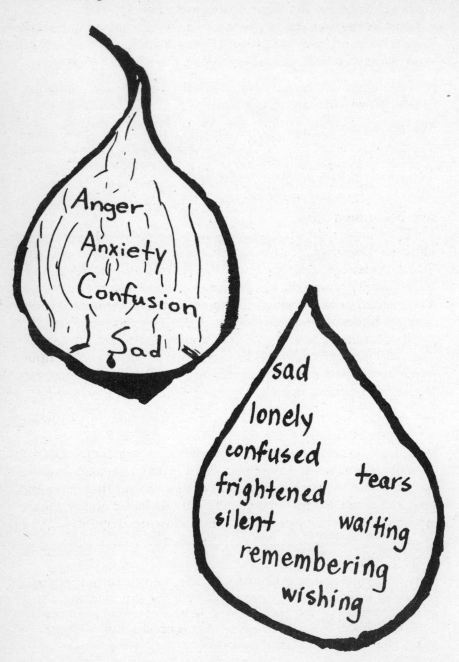

A* Writing letters to someone can be a way for a character to share his or her problems with them and gain self-understanding. It can be like keeping a diary. Challenge students to look for other books in which a character writes to somebody else.

Leigh Botts, for example, writes to a favorite author in Beverly Cleary's *Dear Mr. Henshaw*, and Terry Blanchard writes to his rock superstar hero in Kevin Major's *Dear Bruce Springsteen*.

TEARS: MEMORIES OF THE PAST

We all come to a new home with a host of memories. Nam-Huong is no exception. A sudden noise, an unexpected smell, a certain color—all bring back a flood of memories. Have the students locate some of the ones in this book, such as, "Miss Lily's perfume is like her uncle's garden," or, "Riding on the bike is like being on a trishaw."

The reluctance or apparent inability of newly arrived youngsters from troubled parts of the world to talk is a common trait. The experiences and memories they have of the long trip, perhaps scarcity of food, and sometimes the death of many people shocks them into numbness. If you have friends from Asia who have been though similar experiences to Nam-Huong's, they will, even in adulthood, be reluctant to talk about their past, not wanting to dredge up old ghosts and nightmares once more. In time, the sharing of such memories should be encouraged as it allows the healing process to begin.

A* Read a picture book which illustrates the same cultural shock effect on a child. Michele Maria Surat's *Dragon Child* visually shows the trauma of a young Vietnamese arriving in the United States. Encourage the students to use this book to make a "mood graph" from the character's point of view. After they have the idea, they can construct one for Nam-Huong based on her letters. An example of one appears on the following page.

> **Reflection:**
> What is culture shock? How does it affect some students in our schools when they first come to our country? It is evident right now in children who can't learn yet because of nightmares about the horrors they have witnessed, their sense of insecurity, and the frail emotional state they are in.

Onion Tears: Mood Graph

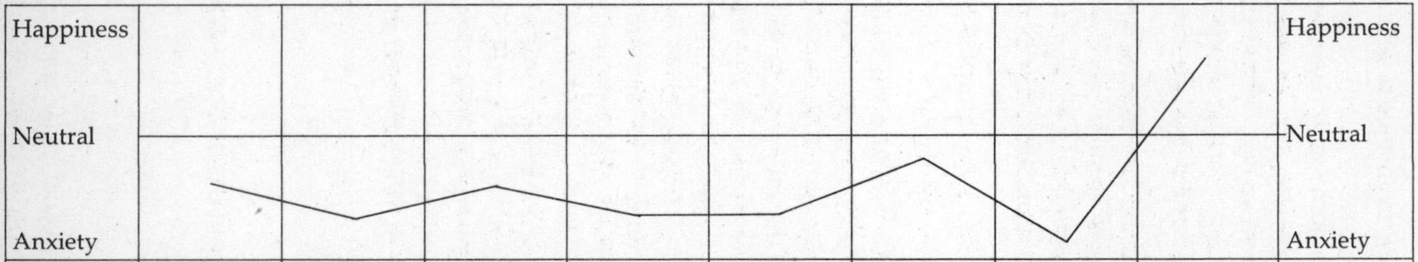
Happiness
Neutral
Anxiety
Happiness
Neutral
Anxiety

	Letter to little yellow canary remem-bering her home, wondering about her mom and dad	Letter to little duck as white as a cloud remem-bering the night that soldiers came, wondering why her family doesn't write	Letter to Mr. Buffalo remem-bering how her dad talked to his animals just like Miss Lily does	Letter to little yellow canary reveals Nam's departure with Grandpa	Letter to little duck as white as a cloud reveals Nam and Grandpa's arrival at the sea	Letter to little yellow canary tells of Nam's walk with Samson	Letter to little yellow canary tells of Nam's and Grandpa's boat trip when Grandpa died	The swallows return north with a message from Nam to her family	

> This book shows us the importance of our emotions, how we need to deal with them openly and not repress them.

The Most Beautiful Place in the World
Ann Cameron

THE STORY

Juan, a seven-year-old Guatemalan boy, is sent to live with his grandmother after his mother remarries and her new husband doesn't want him. He helps his grandmother with selling of arroz con leche and has his own shoeshine stand. In the process he finds out about hard work and the joy of learning. He teaches himself to read.

Ann Cameron has written an unusual book, one which is deceptively simple on the surface yet which speaks volumes about the hardships of daily life and the struggle to get ahead in a developing country.

The strength of this story lies in its changing images of life as seen by Juan. Because of the special pacing of this book it is recommended that it be read aloud by the teacher. In this manner the beauty of the language and the rich imagery will become apparent to listeners.

FOOD FOR THOUGHT

• What are the important scenes in your life?
• What makes a place beautiful?
• What are the special places in your life?
• How important are people in your special places?

A* Encourage the students to find sections of the book which describe visual scenes. They give us a sense of beauty from the child's experience. Some of these are the big house with the fence and the peacock, the lake with lights on it, Grandmother's house, and the fact that Juan remembers the peacock better than he does his father.

Encourage students to find quotes from the book and illustrate them. What is Juan's world really like? There are two sides to it. What place do you think Juan would like to see?

I AM JUAN

A* As you read the book aloud, encourage students to assume the character, feelings, dreams, and reality of Juan. A reader's theatre presentation would be most appropriate to evoke the boy's feelings.

A* Juan is not alone. Children in villages all over the world are determined to change their lives and use the talent they might have. Fernando in his village in Panama in Patricia Maloney Markun's *The Little Painter of Sabana Grande* learns from his teacher how to make paints. Afraid at first that he might not have anything to paint, he follows a hunch to portray the colorful delights of his village. Encourage students to find other books telling about children overcoming tremendous odds to live a better life.

Reflection:
The power of this book lies in the remarkable visual images created by the writer and the fact that we are able to look at the world from the boy's point of view.

Tikta'liktak
James Houston

THE STORY

Tikta'liktak picked the soft warm feathered birds out of the water, and after recovering his arrows, he piled them on the ice and started out after the small bird that had drifted beyond him. With much difficulty, he finally reached it with his harpoon and pulled it to the edge of the ice. When he turned to retrace his steps to the pile of birds, a huge crack had opened in the ice, barring his path. It was too wide to jump. Tikta'liktak realized with horror that he could not return. He was drifting out to sea on a large pan of ice, carried by the rising wind and tide.

Houston's descriptive language for setting and action create a suspenseful survival story about an Inuit boy. He quickly sets the stage, emphasizing Tikta'liktak's respect for his harsh environment and the struggling animals around him.

FOOD FOR THOUGHT

- How does Tikta'liktak survive physically?
- How does he survive mentally? What thought keeps him sane while he is completely alone week after week?
- How does he feel on his return to his family? Why does he approach cautiously? What does this say about Inuit beliefs?
- As city people we are concerned about animal rights. The Inuit of today, as well as Tikta'liktak, hunt to survive. Who actually respects animals? What passages give evidence of Inuit respect?
- How do you feel as you read parts of the book which depict hunting?
- Why do we prefer to buy our meat packaged in plastic on a Styrofoam tray?
- Today we refer to the Eskimo (eaters of raw meat according to other Indians at the time of early European contact) by their true name Inuit (we the people). Why is it important to acknowledge this change of name and attitude towards the First Nations?
- How important is our own name to each of us?

INTRODUCTORY STRATEGY

A* Read aloud *Tikkatou's Journey* by Amanda Loverseed to introduce the concept of journeys, the Inuit world, and closeness of family and nature. As a class, create a story map to follow Tikkatou's route. Point out that Tikta'liktak's journey is extensive, because of the circumstances he finds himself in, and therefore becomes a survival story.

A* After students have read *Tikta'liktak*, partners, individuals, or small groups could create a story map of key events, modelled after the class story map for *Tikkatou's Journey*.

Below the surface appeal of this story lies a deeper layer. Houston's own life with the Inuit for many years gives him credibility and knowledge. Tikta'liktak's story is true to the Inuit outlook on life. Their closeness to animals is exemplified by their hunting methods and respect for their source of survival. Nothing is wasted. One small group of students can post details in key words or phrases which show this. Another small group can web our culture's current uses of/beliefs about animals. Two other groups can compare through discussion. Individual written response to the issue could answer such questions as, "What is important to you?" "Is there a right way to regard animals?" "What compromises do you make regarding animals?"

The issue of survival is presented as a harsh but acceptable reality for Tikta'liktak and the Inuit. Their ingenious use of basics provided by nature is in contrast to our dependence on society for our survival. One small group of students can post details in key words or phrases which show this. Another small group can web our daily survival routine. Two groups may then compare though discussion. Individual written responses to the issue could answer questions such as, "What would be your chances on your own?" "How could you cope alone?" "How would you create shelter, find food?"

CONCLUDING STRATEGIES

It is important that students realize *Tikta'liktak* is a story of long ago. To bridge then and now, read aloud and discuss *Arctic Memories* by Norm Ekoomiak and *Pictures Out of My Life* by Pitseolak. View films such as *Kenojuak: An Eskimo Artist*, which shows James Houston as a member of the Cape Dorset Printmaking Co-operative. Peruse the information book section of the library for current books at the young readers' level.

For an art activity, printmaking is an enjoyable, appropriate experience. James Houston, an artist himself, was instrumental in promoting this art form with the Inuit. The 1.5-centimetre blue insulation Styrofoam could be used for a soapstone carving block as the design can be etched with a thick sketching pencil. Water-based printmaking ink is rolled on sheets of glass, then applied to the carved block to create interesting colors and designs with the paint. As shown in the Kenojuak film the paper is placed, smoothed down, then hung to dry. Subsequent prints are created by rolling more paint on top of the remaining paint on the block. Children should be encouraged to experiment with color and design rather than trying to copy the Inuit format of reproducing many exact, identical prints.

In this way, we begin with their art form, adapt it to our ability level and purpose to complete the circle of learning which started when they adapted a western art form to become among the most revered printmakers because of their unique images, perspective, and style.

Reflection:
More and more we realize that we are on an unsustainable path and need to look in other directions for perspectives to adapt to today's world. Literature can be a cue for discussion when we find rich stories which present other cultures' viewpoint of the world.

Key Books 10+

Number the Stars
Lois Lowry

THE STORY

Two young Danish girls are caught in the turmoil of Copenhagen in World War II. It is only after the Germans close all the shops owned by Jews that Annemarie realizes her friend Ellen is Jewish and may be in trouble. Why does her brother Peter have to visit at night? During the Jewish New Year Ellen comes to live with Annemarie's family as her sister. She arrives just in time, as the Germans are arresting the Jews.

FOOD FOR THOUGHT

Lowry's novel is incredibly rich in its imagery, tension, and depiction of child involvement in wartime activities. It raises many important issues and questions discussed in "Caught in the Shadow of War."

- What is the culture of war?
- What is war's effect on culture?

Number the Stars gives the reader a view of wartime Denmark through the eyes of two girls. The reader will gradually come to realize the broader situation and its implications as specific incidents are related to the two girls.

A* How do the girls gradually become aware of what is happening around them?

A* Find evidence in the book of the girls' view of what is taking place.

As the story unfolds, the friendship of the two girls is strengthened and leads, as it turns out, into a lifelong one. Another powerful novel to share aloud with older students is Hans Peter Richter's *Friedrich*, translated from the German by Edite Kroll. Two young boys, living in the same apartment building, are friends at the start of the war. At first the fact that one is of Jewish background makes no difference. Gradually it does. When Friedrich tries to join the youth movement he is turned down. This is symbolic of what is going to happen—the gradual isolation and rejection of Friedrich and his family.

The same theme of altered friendship is reflected in Doris Orgel's *The Devil in Vienna*. Two girls, one Jewish, are caught in the same situation of external forces pressuring for an end to their friendship. In this case the Jewish parents simply remove their daughter from Vienna for her own "safety."

A comparison of events and attitudes in this trio of novels will result in many hours of beneficial discussion.

CULTURAL TREASURES

The concept of culture in a child's mind is very often associated with human-made objects. This is because such objects are visible expressions of a culture and often thought to be special. Many have particular significance for an individual or family and some may even have histories of their own.

A* Examine the cover of the book and notice that there is a necklace with the Star of David on it. What is the meaning of it? Who does it belong to? What does its significance prove to be in the novel?

A* What other cultural treasures are referred to in the novel?

WAR AND CULTURE

A* If a culture is a set of beliefs which unite a people, encourage the students to find or infer the cultural beliefs of the "Aryan" Danes, the Jewish Danes, and the Germans.

WHAT'S IMPORTANT ANYWAY?

In times of crisis two things are particularly important to all of us. These are friendship and beliefs.

Lowry's book stands as a testament to friendship. It is actually the story of her real-life friend, Annelise Platt, and how she was saved by friends during the war.

A* Encourage students to make a chart/diagram as a visible reminder of the number and strengths of friendships in this book. These range from those between family members to other families to complete strangers united by a mutual set of beliefs.

On the spiritual side, we all need a strong set of beliefs. These may be of a religious nature or they may consist of a personal code of ethics. In this book many individuals are opposed to the Nazi extermination of the Jewish people. They cannot condone or cooperate in such an endeavor, and so they make a conscious decision to help in whatever way they can.

A* Challenge the students to list the people who set out to help the Jewish Danes to escape. Some are with the Resistance, others are watchful, supportive neighbors, others are actively involved in the escape.

A* Role play one of the individuals who helps the Jews to escape. Even those merely mentioned in the novel have a story to tell. By reading and comparing other war novels students can create personalities with beliefs, occupations, and histories of activities. Hold a panel to allow them to tell their stories.

> **Reflection:**
> We need to remind ourselves of the golden rule of doing unto others as we would have them do unto us.
>
> It is important for individuals to stand up for what they believe. Many people do this during times of war. Today, helping others is a strong impulse in many people; we witness them helping others to flee from danger, welcoming new immigrants, and being warm, accepting human beings.

A Jar of Dreams
Yoshiko Uchida

THE STORY

For eleven-year-old Rinko, growing up in California as a Japanese-American during the Depression is often difficult. She feels inferior to her schoolmates and she rejects the cultural aspects of her life which single her out as different. Her family faces prejudice and even violence from some members of the community. When Aunt Waka arrives from Japan for a visit, she acts as a catalyst for change in the lives of all members of Rinko's family. Rinko gains a new perspective on her cultural heritage and in the process learns to value herself as an individual.

FOOD FOR THOUGHT

- How much of who we are is a product of our beliefs about how others perceive us?
- What parts of ourselves do we reject because they don't fit arbitrary standards set (explicitly or implicitly) by our society?
- What happens to someone who feels they must say goodbye to important parts of their cultural heritage in order to be accepted?

Mama tells Rinko that her dust-covered trunk contains "her Japanese self—everything in the world she'd owned when she came to America to marry Papa." She shares some of the contents: old school notebooks, family photos, Japanese clothing. Then she carefully puts them away, explaining that she doesn't need these things anymore. Rinko is disturbed. She begins to see her mother in a different light, believing that "part of her was locked up in her big trunk, never to get out."

A* Have students consider this idea. What kind of pressure might this "locked-up" feeling exert on an individual? In what ways might such pressure affect an individual's behavior? Is it only Mama whose Japanese self appears locked up?

A* Challenge students to find quotations which support the idea that Rinko feels pressure to lock herself away from her Japanese heritage in order to be accepted.

When Rinko is excused from Japanese Language School for health reasons: "I couldn't have been more thrilled, because going to Japanese Language School after regular school was just one more thing to make me different from my classmates." (p. 13)

When Aunt Waka gives Rinko a kimono Rinko promises to try it on later, but confesses, "What I really had in mind was that I'd put it in Mama's trunk in the basement with all her kimonos and probably never look at it again." (p. 53)

On Aunt Waka's Japanese style of dress: "And how were we ever going to take her anyplace if she went everywhere in a kimono?" (p.58)

On choosing a picnic spot in the park: "We'd pick a nice isolated spot where no one would see us eating riceballs and pickles with our chopsticks." (p. 104)

Rinko repeatedly expresses a wish to "just disappear." Her soft voice at school and her poor posture are but two outward indicators of her poor self-concept.

A* Have students think about situations in their own lives when they have felt really good about themselves and situations when they have not felt good about themselves. Invite them to web some of the outward indicators of such feelings. Encourage them to recognize and be sensitive to these outward indicators.

My **Positive Self-Concept**
I can admit failures
I learn from mistakes
I am able to accept praise
I have a confident manner
I am able to laugh at myself
I have a sure voice
I am not easily defeated, I keep trying
I have a proud carriage
I keep my head up, chin out

My **Negative Self-Concept**
I have poor posture
I keep my head down, slouched over
I'm unable to accept praise or blame
My manner lacks confidence
I have a soft voice
I am easily defeated and give up

A JAR OF DREAMS

At the end of the novel, Rinko feels a new pride in herself. She believes that her life can be more positive and she resolves to start a "jar of dreams," in which she will save money to fulfil dreams such as visiting Aunt Waka in Japan.

A* Each student could create his or her own "jar of dreams" by using magazine pictures as well as hand-drawn illustrations and words on a large, jar-shaped piece of tag board (or around a large pickle jar). The resulting collage should depict some of their hopes and dreams for the future. This could have either a personal or a world focus. The dream jars could be shared and displayed around the classroom.

Reflection:
All people need to feel a sense of pride in their cultural heritage in order to maintain a positive self-concept. By celebrating a rich mosaic of culture with our students, we affirm the value of each individual, thus contributing to the development of self-esteem. We can make a difference.

Underground to Canada

Barbara Smucker

THE STORY

Set in the "deep south" of the mid-1800s this is a fictional story about two young slave girls, Liza and Julilly, their attempt to escape to Canada via the Underground Railroad, and their eventual success. Figuratively, the events of the story take place completely "under the surface" — underground. The story details their desperate, fearful journey.

"Who, Mammy?" is the naive, plaintive question asked by Julilly, after Mammy Sally fearfully tells her, "June Lilly, child....You know the slave trader's in our town. Some of the slaves is to be sold."

Unaware of the personal trauma she will have to endure, Julilly is forced to face the world alone, deprived of psychological, emotional, and physical protection and torn from her mother's reassuring love.

FOOD FOR THOUGHT

- Are any of us completely free?
- Will humankind ever rid itself of tortuous actions toward one another?

LET MY PEOPLE GO

Julilly is sold. She finds herself taken from the "friendly" Henson plantation near Richmond, Virginia to the dreaded Riley plantation near Vicksburg, Mississippi. There, life is worse than imaginable, as the slaves have to live and work in unbearable conditions. They are kept in a state of constant starvation, forced to work from sun-up to sun-down in oppressive heat, deprived of water, clothed only with rags, and living in cramped shacks far from the grand plantation mansion.

As early Biblical writings indicate, Moses pleaded to the Egyptian Pharaoh to "let his people go." The enslaved culture was suffering and someone had to be the spokesperson and demand freedom. Throughout history, we witness outstanding men and women who fought for and dedicated their lives to achieving basic human rights for oppressed peoples, including freedom from torture and the opportunity to exist peaceably in the context of a particular culture and religion.

A* Students could undertake a study of their family history (roots), including a family tree. Research into the culture of their ancestry could lead to discoveries about the freedoms and restrictions people lived with during a given historical period. Were there any heroes in the culture? Grouping could vary, depending upon the cultural backgrounds of students. For instance, those with similar cultural backgrounds could work together in pairs.

A* A timeline could be developed tracing a family move (route) from the country of origin to the present dwelling place.

A* The route the family took could be plotted on a "Family History" map and a short narrative written to explain each point on the map, like storymapping. A paragraph could accompany the map, focusing on signs of culture that indicate the original "roots" of the family, such as clothing, cooking utensils, art objects, religious containers, etc. that identify them as being part of a particular culture.

A* Students will discover that culture is not easily defined. A student may be of a particular ethnic ancestry, for instance Chinese, but have spent their entire life in a country with a completely different culture such as one in South America, and feel more Spanish than Chinese, especially if able to speak only Spanish. Discuss whether culture is more a matter of mind and heart than outward appearances and ancestral lineage.

A* For students unable to trace their historical roots, recent moves from one home to another could be described. These moves contain in miniature the elements of larger continental moves and are equally important. Uprooting is difficult in any circumstances.

A GLOBAL PERSPECTIVE

Students need to be aware that slavery has not stopped. It continues in various forms around the world. And, as always, children bear the brunt of this tragedy and suffer the most. To ensure that students have a global perspective is to inform them of the entire range of actions and behaviors that rule and govern the lives of people, regardless of language, culture, and race. In dealing with sensitive issues, graphic details are not necessary, but awareness of one's audience and a specific educational goal must remain foremost in the minds of educators.

Have we been bought or sold against our will? Emotionally or physically? Desperate athletes sell their bodies in the quest for a gold medal. They use steroids and other drugs. Unable to cope with life, some people sell themselves in exchange for damaging drugs like crack and cocaine. Addictions are rampant.

- Do they begin as self-inflicted steps to victory over perceived weaknesses?
- Or are they imposed upon unwary people as a means of control?

Gambling in all its forms begins by choice, yet in many people rapidly gains a foothold in their lives. Is it a form of self-slavery? Anorexia and bulimia indicate an obsession with and type of slavery to food. Julilly is a slave physically, but she retains a freedom of spirit that not even the cruelest of slave-traders can annihilate. She can't be broken. Teachers are encouraged to build self-esteem in students and give them the assurance that their inner spirit and strength of character will always be their fortress. For many students, this may be the only "Rock of Gibralter" they experience in their lives.

A* Using articles from newspapers and magazines students could develop a web or chain on "Types of Personal Slavery." Working in cooperative groups of four including an above-average student, two average students, and one below-average student the groups could find articles that discuss various concerns and divide them into two basic categories, external and internal. There may be overlapping, as some issues are not clearly defined and may contain elements of both external and internal factors. After information is collected and transferred to the web, students can be asked to write paragraphs relating to specific areas, such as societal slavery, personal addictions, the role of media and advertising in promoting certain addictions, etc. Each group could be required to hand in a paper containing all paragraphs written by members of the group, plus an introduction and conclusion.

Key Books 11+

Kiss the Dust
Elizabeth Laird

THE STORY

Tara, a Kurdish teenager, is jolted out of her childhood happiness when the Iraqi government starts to actively persecute the Kurdish resistance movement during the Iran-Iraq war. Her family escapes to safety in the Kurdistan hills and then through the mountains to refugee camps in Iran. The war continues to rage between the two countries and the family realizes they will not be able to re-establish the quality of life they had enjoyed in Iraq. Through distant family contacts and a fortuitous political connection, Tara's family manages to emigrate to London. Starting over again is another challenge but they are full of optimism because of the opportunities offered by their new home.

FOOD FOR THOUGHT

- When should parents tell children the truth about what is happening in troubled times?
- How do we know it is time to change?
- How do we react to change?

KISS THE DUST

The title is a powerful one. Encourage students to brainstorm about what it could mean. Some possibilities might include the following:

- Surviving in a desert area
- Death—dust to dust
- Coming back to the homeland after a long time, kissing the ground as the Pope does when he visits places.

IT'S TIME TO LEAVE...

An underlying theme of the book is that people's lives change whether they are ready or not. In this story Tara and indeed her mother aren't ready to change, can't accept the fact that it is indeed time to change, and probably never fully realize that they have changed. Only later in the novel is there any evidence that Tara is aware that she herself has changed.

How do people change? Why?

SAFETY PLOT

Tara reaches "safety" four times, yet the first three, although initially comforting, prove untenable refuges from danger.
1. When she sees violence in the street (a young boy is shot), she runs into her house to get away.
2. When the family realizes that their home is under observation, the mother and children flee to their village.
3. When the mountain village is bombed, the family realizes that they must flee over the mountains to Iran.
4. When the family realizes that the refugee camp in Iran is only full of deceit, threat, and illness, they know it is time to flee to London.

A* Students could plot this rollercoaster flight graphically with labels and artwork, incorporating details highlighting:
a. causes of comfort/security;
b. introduction of unsettling new causes for concern.

A* Speculate on how this pattern might continue in London. What could be the downside of going there?

"I'VE CHANGED!"

A* Challenge students to make a list of incidents or quotations from the book which support this statement.

A* Relate the book to the readers themselves. Have they ever changed? Have the students construct their own timelines highlighting important changes in their own lives up to the present—for instance, the birth of a sibling, moves, leaving friends, making new friends, significant family changes such as divorce, death, new challenges and achievements. What changes have been the most significant ones for them? Why?

The use of a confidential personal journal might be appropriate for this activity.

THE STRUGGLE OF THE KURDS

What do the students know about the Kurds? Where can they find out more? Around a large map of Kurdistan, students can post information they have found.

An excellent article by Christopher Hitchens, "Struggle of the Kurds," is to be found in *National Geographic*, August 1992 (Vol. 182, No.2, p. 33-61). In it he makes the following observations that bring a new dimension to an appreciation of the novel.

He comments that there are 25 million Kurds, mostly Suni Muslims, one of the largest ethnic groups without a state of its own. Three million Kurds live in a 15,000-square-mile region of Iraq that they call Free Kurdistan. The Kurdish guerrillas are called peshmerga, or "one who has made an understanding with death."

"Since the mid-1970s President Saddam Hussein's campaign to eradicate the Kurdish resistance movement has claimed 4,000 towns and villages and more than 100,000 lives."

Despite being dispersed, all Kurds have certain fundamental similarities. They are survivors.

Reflection:

It is interesting to note that Tara can never define herself or her home, but only the spirit within her. This is also true of the peoples of the Basque and Jewish cultures (the latter prior to the creation of Israel). Could it be true of other cultures?

- What is the importance of having a national identity?
- How does it impact on the individual?
- What makes us who we are?
- How can we hang onto the important aspects of our own cultural heritage?

Star Fisher
Laurence Yep

THE STORY

When sixteen-year-old Joan and her family arrive in a small West Virginia town in 1927 to open a laundry, they become the first Chinese-Americans in the region. Being the eldest, she shares the family's struggles to gain acceptance and friendship and to overcome the prejudice and ignorance present in the small town.

Embedded in the story is a retelling of the Chinese legend of the Starfisher, the golden kingfisher forced to remain earthbound as wife of the man who stole and hid her golden cloak. Forever yearning to join her sisters as they soar through the heavens "fishing for stars" she remains captive on earth. The sadness and longing experienced by this bird-woman are paralleled by Joan's feelings.

FOOD FOR THOUGHT

Everyone experiences at some time a sense of alienation.
- Are our stereotyped ideas of other cultural groups true?
- How willing are we to take risks for friendship?
- Will we stand up in defense of a minority?
- How effective is our communication with others?
- How important is our family to us?
- Why is it sometimes frustrating for young people to deal with parents?

THE TITLE

Laurence Yep has selected an obvious, yet intriguing title for his novel. Students could be encouraged to speculate what the story might be about because of it: fishermen? starfish? counting stars? space travel? California?

CULTURAL MARKERS

With the arrival of this family in a strange town, the author provides us with many markers that are evidence of both Chinese and American cultures. Challenge students to find these in the text, compiling a portrait of those things which are important for traditional families, both Chinese and American. For example, Joan's father is a scholar who writes poetry.

Is the racist writing on the fence, telling the family to go home, a different type of cultural marker?

CULTURAL ENCOUNTERS

The book is filled with episodes through which the reader comes in contact with the culture of another group. This is exactly the stuff that readers' theatre or story drama are designed for. Some appropriate scenes for dramatization include: the family's arrival at the station and their encounter with a redneck; their arrival at their new home; and tea with Miss Lucy.

A further approach would be to have the students, in role, form a tableau of a scene. Then, as you touch them lightly on the shoulder, they each come to life and tell what is happening in the scene and how they feel about it.

Much of the culture is passed on by Joan's mother. Is she a traditional stereotype? Why can't she cook? She provides a stark contrast to the role of women like Miss Lucy.

Joan's mother recognizes the importance of family, and she also has sympathy for Miss Lucy, who has no relatives, and Miss Lucy's network of friends—her real family. She likes the idea of their working together and being "cooking cousins" because this is a way that she can befriend Miss Lucy and include her as part of her Chinese family, giving both of them the friendship and support they need.

CHARACTER ENCOUNTERS

Laurence Yep is a master at creating intriguing characters. We get a first glimpse of them through the eyes of Joan as she rides the trains to West Virginia.

Spunky Emily, her younger sister, is a favorite with readers as it is she who is willing to take on the world. Does she, perhaps, feel more "American" than her older siblings and parents, less caught between two cultural shadows?

Joan's mother is feisty. She looks forward to change and encourages it in her husband even though she insists that the children speak Chinese at home. She understands, however, her husband's need to express himself aesthetically.

Encourage students to become one of the characters, constructing profiles for each of their likes, dislikes, preferences, fears, habits, etc. The relationships among them are interesting and detailed, with Joan at the hub.

CHARACTERIZATION: JOHARI WINDOW

This "window" was developed by Joseph Luft and Harry Ingram as an awareness model for group processes. It relates to what we and others know about ourselves. There are four quadrants in it.

1. The public self	2. The blind self
3. The private self	4. The unknown self

The first quadrant or public self contains what is known about an individual's behaviors and motives by themselves and others. The second quadrant or blind self lists those observations made by outsiders about habits of the individual, those things the individual is not aware of, such as mannerisms or verbal cues. The third area or private self consists of those traits/beliefs that are known only to the individual and must be inferred by other characters or the reader. The fourth area or unknown self includes information which is unknown by both the individual and outsiders and must, therefore, be inferred by the reader.

Have students construct a Johari Window for Joan; working in small groups of two to five is more enjoyable and results in more insightful discussion. Put the finished windows on a chart and then share with the entire class.

Joan's Johari Window

1. Intelligent Strong-willed	2. Calm Confident Has power and strength
3. Questions parents Embarrassed at their poverty Uses star fisher story as her hope	4. Co-dependence (*mother and daughter*) Is a survivor

THE METAPHOR OF THE BIRD

The embedding of the star fisher legend in the story gives rise to many other references to birds. Encourage the students to find these for themselves and to note why they are used.

"When I saw this woman, she reminded me of a bird." (p. 13)

"When Bernice grinned a welcome at me, it made all the freckles on her cheeks rise up like a flock of birds." (p. 57)

"I suppose when the star fisher's daughter had gone for a walk in their village, the neighbors had smirked in just the same way. Moving through the hallways, I felt as if I were marked by a drop of blood from a falling feather." (p. 63)

"More and more, it seemed as if Papa had brought us into a trap. Looking up at the sky, I raised my arms and wished I could fly up to the moon. Or just away. Anyplace." (p. 84)

The story of the star fisher, the child who belongs on earth and in the sky, is beautifully told and applied by Joan to her own and Bernice's situations—trying to fit in, make friends, and be accepted. Everyone, even Miss Lucy, has at some time felt alone or misplaced. This assembly of intriguing characters gives us a chance to look at our own reactions.

- Do we fight like Emily?
- Play ball like Bobby?
- Rely on philosophy and pride?
- Scrub away negative and insulting comments on the fence?

The embedded tale allows the characters in the novel to escape into their imagination to rekindle their ability to cope in the real world of racism and prejudice. It brings the story to another level—symbolic of a trapped, yet hopeful family.

Encourage students to read Mollie Hunter's *The Stranger Came Ashore*, in which Old Da and Robbie tell the reader about Selkie folklore.

Reflection:

Stereotypes such as "Chinese children can't speak English," "All women can cook," and "Scholars don't run laundries" are false.

In order to truly help others, special sensitivity is required so that we may see into their innermost beings without judging them according to false social perceptions. Whether it be at the church social, in pie baking, or in the laundry business, communication is vital.

The Curses of Third Uncle
Paul Yee

THE STORY

Canadian-born Lillian Ho is embarrassed by the old-world customs which set Vancouver's Chinese community apart from mainstream west coast society in 1909. Then her father, a supporter of Dr. Sun Yat-Sen and the Chinese Revolution, disappears while on a mysterious mission. Lillian discovers that his younger brother, Third Uncle, has betrayed both her father and the revolution. She travels to Revelstoke hoping to find her father before Third Uncle sends her family back to China.

Though she is unable to save her father's life, she and Dr. Sun prevent Third Uncle from selling information to enemies of the revolution. Lillian's mother decides the family will remain in Canada, and Lillian acquires a new pride in her heritage and resolves to work toward realizing her father's dream.

FOOD FOR THOUGHT

- What happens when one's loyalties are divided?
- Is loyalty to a cause more important than loyalty to individuals?
- What conflicts exist between first-generation and second-

generation immigrant family members, and what causes these conflicts?

- Are subtle forms of prejudice more damaging than blatant racism?
- What has been the history of Canada's treatment of its Chinese citizens?

LILLIAN'S PERCEPTION OF THE CHINESE

Initially, Lillian is embarrassed by old-world customs which draw attention to cultural differences between the Chinese and the Caucasians.

A* Encourage students to find evidence in the book to support this statement. The following are examples.

"Three Chinese stood out from the crowd with long pigtails dangling down behind their Chinese-style jackets...As people turned and stared, Lillian's face reddened..." 'Can't they at least step into the shade where people won't see them?' " (p. 2-3)

"If she weren't Chinese and her family wasn't so poor, Lillian thought enviously, she would be wearing a dress like that, too!" (p. 6)

"More than half the car's occupants were Chinese men...Lillian scanned their faces to see if Papa was among them. Then she wished they would hush themselves before the white people started to complain. Why couldn't the Chinese read or smoke quietly like the whites were doing? Why couldn't the Chinese hold regular conversations in low voices?" (p. 62)

A* Yiwen tells Lillian that her attitudes about the Chinese have been formed because she only knows the bad things about China. Challenge students to examine the book for evidence to support or refute this, and hold a panel discussion on the issue.

A QUESTION OF LOYALTY

In this story, loyalty is a key issue—loyalty to one's family, to one's cultural heritage, to a cause or a country. Sometimes these loyalties conflict, causing tension and disharmony.

A* Invite students to find and summarize examples of conflicting loyalties in the book.

Mrs. Ho, for instance, believes that her husband is being irresponsible in placing his commitment to the revolution ahead of his commitment to the family. She feels he has abandoned his family to "play revolution." (p. 26)

Lillian's mother opposes her plan to escort a young Chinese immigrant to Revelstoke because she feels Lillian should help her own family first. (p. 52)

On the train to Revelstoke, Lillian is upset when Yiwen changes into comfortable Chinese clothes. She tells her, "But it's different here....We can't do everything we want. We can't upset the whites." (p. 63)

Reflection:
Sometimes our perception of a particular culture, even our own, is clouded because we consider only its negative features. What can we do to obtain a more balanced perspective? How can we share this with others?

The Eternal Spring of Mr. Ito
Sheila Garrigue

THE STORY

It is 1941, and British guest child Sara Warren is living with her aunt and uncle in Vancouver for the duration of the war. She develops a close friendship with the family's Japanese-Canadian gardener, Mr. Ito, whose gentle philosophy about the eternal renewal of life comforts Sara when the chaos of the world threatens to overwhelm her.

The attack on Pearl Harbor and its devastating consequences for west coast people of Japanese ancestry is personalized for Sara as a result of her relationship with Mr. Ito. She is faced with a moral dilemma as she endeavors to secretly maintain a friendship which many in her society would consider unpatriotic.

FOOD FOR THOUGHT

- Do we realize that as human beings, we are more alike than different? We all experience the same emotions and have the same need for acceptance and understanding.

- How can fear and propaganda fuel an attitude of discrimination in difficult times?
- What happens to a society when the voice of prejudice dominates?
- How can the harmony of nature be reflected in human relationships?
- How can one individual find the courage to do what is right, despite an attitude of discrimination sanctioned by society?
- What value do we place on friendship?
- How can our beliefs strengthen us in times of darkness?

THE DILEMMA

Sara is faced with a personal dilemma when she weighs her own perception of what is right against the discriminatory attitude of those around her towards Canadians of Japanese descent.

A* Encourage students to find quotations from the book which show how members of society reacted to the Japanese-Canadian population after the attack on Pearl Harbor.

When Sara's aunt defends the Itos against the angry rock throwing mob on Powell Street: "They've sure got you fooled, sister...You'd better get out of Japtown or you'll be tarred with the same brush!" (p. 49)

A Mountie, alert to violence against Japanese: "Let 'em go ahead, I say— my brother-in-law's a sailor on the Arizona." (p. 49-50)

Uncle Duncan: "Ito, you are to pack up your stuff and leave. I don't want you near this house again!" (p. 57)

At the streetcar stop, when Sara and Mr. Ito's daughter are seen together: "What's a Jap doing out among decent people?" "It shouldn't be allowed! But we'll be rid of them soon... Some people aren't too choosy about the people they associate with!" (p. 85, 86)

A* How do these sentiments make Sara's choice a difficult one?

A* A short dramatization of quotations like the above could be a powerful method of presenting the frightening face of racism.

A* Students might write letters or journal entries, in role as Sara, describing her own confusion as she listens to these reactions.

Mr. Ito shows Sara his most cherished bonsai tree, the aiguro-matsu, part black pine and part red. It was given to him by his father when he left Japan for Canada as a symbol of his dual heritage, Japanese and Canadian.

Rising up proudly from the rock in which it is embedded, roots totally exposed, its survival is a source of wonder to Sara.

A* Have students look for references in the book which reflect the importance of the aiguro-matsu to Sara.
• How does her understanding of it change?
• What does it come to represent to her?

PERSONAL SYMBOLS

A* Students might design a personal symbol of their own cultural heritage (a two- or three-dimensional representation) and share it with their classmates.

Reflection:
Have we learned anything since World War II? Prejudice threatens harmony in our world, and in our own communities, today. How can we learn to help one another along the road to enlightenment?

Homesick: My Own Story
Jean Fritz

THE STORY

This memoir spans two years in the author's childhood in China during its transition from feudal empire to Communist republic. She writes many letters to relatives living in America, and longs for the day when she will live with her grandmother in West Virginia and attend regular grade 8 at a real American school. There is always an uneasiness present, as revolution is just around the corner, and Jean and her family seem to be caught in its throes.

- How true is the statement that "Home is where the heart is"?
- Is there a deep longing in each of us to "be at home" emotionally and psychologically as well as physically?
- Will changing our names (as Jean wants to) make us feel more at home?
- Can we be *homesick* for a place we have never seen, but only imagined?
- How can a new immigrant create a "home away from home" and be truly happy?
- Are many new immigrants giving up their "feeling of home" in order to provide a new and better one for their children?
- What cultural images establish a sense of home?

HOMESICK: A LONGING TO BELONG (WHERE IS HOME?)

Jean Fritz lets us know she wants to be wholly American, but also leaves us with images that she cherishes from China. People like Lin Nai Nai, her Chinese Amah (nursemaid), love her dearly and show her this in special ways. Lin Nai Nai is also homesick. She has left her unfaithful husband and as a result is ostracized by her family. Never once does she stop longing to go home to Wuchang and be reunited with her family. Her chance comes at last, but she is bitterly disappointed when her father (although starving) rejects her offer of food and reconciliation and does not allow her to see the rest of her family. Jean is moved when she witnesses Lin Nai Nai's distraught state after the attempted visit.

A* Lead students in a trip down memory lane to discuss their beginnings — their family dwelling places.
- Do any remember their first home?
- Are they still living in it?
- If so, what are their earliest memories of it?

- If students are recent immigrants, what was their home like in their country of birth?

Should the first home be too difficult to remember, perhaps an important impression is still alive. Draw out student responses in an emotionally stable setting and validate all answers.

A* Students could discuss Jean's reaction to these questions, finding evidence in the novel for her views or implied views.

A* They could represent their home by creating a floor plan, drawing, or partial sketch of the important impressions left on their minds. The plan could be two-dimensional, or take the form of a sculpture.

WHAT'S IN A NAME?

A* Encourage students to investigate the importance of their names, consulting a name dictionary to find meaning for each. Does having a different name make us a different person? What does Jean think?

Jean desperately wants to change her name. She wants a long name because "Jean" is too short and doesn't allow enough room for a unique personality and a life filled with anything other than goodness. Would she feel more American if her parents had called her Marjorie?

A* Conduct a discussion of these ideas.
- Have students not always felt that goodness was required of them by adults in their life?
- Do students feel required to don personalities suited to people other than themselves?
- Do we take time to look "beneath the surface," and discover what's in others' heart of hearts?

A* Name posters: partner students together, encouraging them to get to know each other. Have them web or chart the interests, outstanding personal qualities, meaning of name, etc. of their partners. Include a photograph of the pairs on each poster and a sample of "Name Art."

REMEMBERING: A TUG AT THE HEART

We all have good and not so good memories of the past. When

we leave a familiar place we feel a tugging at the heart. Many images come to mind, and mixed emotions seem the order of the day. A virtual tug-of-war takes place in the innermost being of anyone who uproots and settles elsewhere, even if it's only a short distance away. The mind and heart know no boundaries of time and space. Distance is relative.

A* Encourage students to recall Jean's lingering images of China that are dear to her. These include:

- jogging rickshas
- chestnut vendors
- water buffalo
- grey-coated soldiers
- Shanghai skyline
- pagodas
- bluebells
- bare-bottomed little boys
- the smells of China—food cooking

Memories make us feel part of forever. Encourage the students to make a visual representation of Jean's memories, or their own.

> **Reflection:**
> Who are we? What validates and defines our existence is vital to our emotional well-being. A longing to belong tugs at all of our hearts and a feeling of "connectedness" to a name, a place, a country, a lifetime of memories is vital to our mental and physical health.

Key books 12 +

Park's Quest
Katherine Paterson

THE STORY

As Parkington Waddell Broughton the Fifth approaches his twelfth birthday, his determination to know more about his father intensifies. Park knows that his father was an American bomber pilot killed in the Vietnamese conflict. He knows that paternal relatives live on an ancestral farm in Virginia, and he knows that it hurts his mother to discuss her past. Due to Park's reluctance to cause his mother pain, he has previously resisted urges to demand information from her. But as the Vietnam Memorial

Wall is unveiled in Washington, Park is spurred into action.

Park's visit to his father's family home serves to pit him against the diminutive, feisty Thanh. At first believed by Park to be an adopted "cousin," Thanh proves to be his half-sister, a child of his own father and the refugee Vietnamese woman his uncle chose to sponsor, protect, and then marry.

This knowledge allows Park insight into his mother's emotional turmoil, causes him to contemplate the issues of guilt, forgiveness, responsibility, and prejudice, and ultimately helps him to redefine his concept of family.

FOOD FOR THOUGHT

What might serve to be the genesis of personal feelings of prejudice? Find evidence of the following:

a. Blame of a specific culture/race for a personal loss; e.g., death or disease of a loved-one.

Thanh? What kind of a name was that? There were lots of Orientals in his school, mostly refugees. Vietnamese, he decided, or Cambodian. They all looked alike to him—the people who had killed his father. (p. 63)

b. Fear of the inability to compete successfully against a member of a different culture.

Referring to milking cows: "Geek Geeeek. geek geeek. Got you. Frank did know how to keep this little barn cat in her place. Park loved it... He didn't care. It wasn't a race, Frank said. Besides, with a little practice he'd be faster than she was anyhow." (p. 84)

What confusion do well-meaning parents bestow on their children in an attempt to protect them from learning about the harsher realities of life? What evidence is found in the novel?

a. The assumption/hope that children may never ask for "sensitive" information.

"Other people have fathers every day. Can't I have a little piece of mine?"
"He died ten years ago."
"Then tell me about him," he begged her stiff body. "Please, Mom, I really need to know." (p. 35)

b. The expectation that no other knowledgeable adult will "spill the beans."

" I'm sorry," he said. "Am I talking out of turn? I just assumed your mother told you."
" Told me what?" He could hardly get the words out.
"You didn't know that she divorced Park?" (p. 106)

c. The failure to see that lack of information can cause children to fantasize and hence create faulty illusions.

He wasn't a farmer. He was a pilot—a bomber pilot—totally in control of a gigantic plane, high above the world. He didn't go around watching for cow shit. (p. 60)

By glamorizing his father's memory, Park is less able to deal with the reality of this man's life; his liaison with a Vietnamese woman, his fathering of a half-sister, his inability to choose between his two families.

FOCUS: QUESTS

Like the medieval knights portrayed in the literature he loves, Park sets out on a quest, a noble crusade to seek out the hidden facts of his father's life and to reclaim his birthright, a treasure stolen from him so long ago by the pain-ridden silence of his mother.

Park's ordeals are tempered in their intensity by his ability to relate his problems to heroic figures of his cultural literature. It can also be said that he creates the unknown personality of his father, and an image of his ideal self, by superimposing his experiences onto the legendary feats of the knights of old. He has a quest, a holy grail to reclaim, a family seat to preserve. He encounters a damsel who could be either Morgana or Guinevere, and he jousts with dragons and black knights—his fears and ignorance of his past.

A* Have a group discussion of the interpretation of the text from several students' viewpoints. The discussion could focus on questions such as:
• What defines a hero?
• Under what circumstances would a person risk the loss of life for a cause?

- Do different societies and cultures place differing degrees of importance on certain character traits?
- How does folklore of other cultures reflect epitomes of behaviors? How realistic are these ideas in the light of modern times?

FOCUS: MEMORIALS

Park's quest is inspired by his visit to the Vietnam War Memorial in Washington, D.C.

A* Encourage the students to explore the concept of memorials. Why do we have them? Who decides? For whom? Gary Paulsen's novel *The Monument* raises many relevant questions as to the appropriateness of such memorial statements.

A* How do war memorials reflect cultural ideas and heritage? Research the symbolism of the sculptures found at the following:
- Ottawa's cenotaph
- Volgograd's Mother Russia
- Hiroshima's Peace Park
- Washington's Arlington Cemetery
- Paris' Arc de Triomphe
- Rome's ancient forum (the portals)

Reflection:

Memories can serve to uplift people, to bring focus and direction to their present lives. On the other hand, memories can haunt them, becoming debilitating impediments to personal growth.

We have some control over which memories we see in technicolor, and which we shove back into the far recesses of our minds. Perhaps this control affords us the ability to create a very personal definition of ourselves, one not influenced by the opinions of others. One's memories are one's exclusive domain.

Shabanu, Daughter of the Wind

Suzanne Fisher Staples

THE STORY

Life in the hot winds of Pakistan's Cholistan Desert is brought to life by a lively young girl, who takes us into her daily existence with enthusiasm, delight, and acceptance. As a twelve-year-old she enjoys her desert home, then quietly, as she matures, she realizes she is growing into a woman, and in helping to prepare for her older sister's marriage, she must face the prospect of her own.

FOOD FOR THOUGHT

- What does freedom mean to each of us?
- What is the role of the veil?
- How different are gender roles in other cultures?

DAUGHTER OF THE WIND

Writers often make use of subtitles to intrigue the reader yet at the same time enhance the interpretation of the story. When asked what the connotation might be for this subtitle, students replied:

- It was a windy country.
- She travelled a lot.
- She was flighty.
- She was a free spirit.
- She was independent.

THE LAND OF THE WIND

So much of one's cultural heritage is dependent on the immediate environment. This book offers readers an opportunity to sense what living in the desert is really like. It does not take too many pages before student readers are aware that they have entered a desert-based culture and the harshness of the environment has dictated, over the generations, culturally accepted behavior such as a nomadic lifestyle and arranged marriages. Young readers need an opportunity to visualize the setting and should be encouraged to find in the book images and facts which characterize desert life.

A* What passages in the book tell about the desert or imply conditions there? Discuss.

A* Encourage students to bring pictures from information books or travel brochures to extend their understanding of life in the desert. Design a collage on the bulletin board.

A* This story takes place in the dry environment of Pakistan. Where else in the world are there deserts with nomadic peoples?

A* How hot is hot? Let students consult references to find average daily temperatures in desert regions. A comparison with night temperatures would show how extreme the temperature variations are.

Suzanne Staples has a sense of love, wonder, and respect for this land of dunes, and it shows in her many descriptive passages. The desert is presented as a land of contrasts. Students can be encouraged to find selections to show the contrasts.

"The winter sky is hazed with dust. There has been no rain in nearly two years, and the heat of the Cholistan Desert is as wicked as if it were summer. Phulan walks with her eyes down, her feet shuffling, kicking up puffs of sand that is light as dust." (p. 1-2)

After the storm: "As suddenly as it began, the storm is over. The air is calm and cool. The storm has buried all signs of civilization. Outside, the desert has been rearranged. Unfamiliar dunes roll where the land used to lie flat. Stands of shrub and thorn trees are no more. Nothing looks the same." (p. 114)

After the rain: "The air is clear—I can smell the sweet absence of dust. The sand sparkles like water, though the early morning breeze has dried it to powder again. Tiny purple flowers cover the ground, where two days ago there was nothing but camel thorn. The winter sky is blue-green above the lavender line that rims the horizon." (p. 9)

A* What other examples of contrast in the physical setting can students find?

A* How are these contrasts reflected in the culture (e.g., the treatment of women, or the notion of shutr keena, "camel vengeance," as it applies to men)?

A* Art activities, including sand-painting, which focus on texture can help students capture the visual characteristics of the landscape.

WATER

A crucial lifeline of the desert is a readily available supply of water for both humans and animals. During the dry season, families must be on the move trying to locate sufficient supplies of water. This need comes through very clearly in the book as all characters are profoundly water-conscious.

A* Encourage students to keep track of all the liquid that they drink in one day. By doing this for a few days, and charting the results, you will raise the level of awareness of just how much water we do use. Try going for a few hours without water and see what the feeling is like. Research the effects of water dehydration.

THIS IS MY LIFE!

Staples' book offers a unique view of nomad life through the eyes of a twelve-year-old girl. The role of women in this society is a key aspect of the novel. What Shabanu faces as part of her normal life will intrigue young North American readers. Time should be spent trying to have students see the setting and events of the book through Shabanu's eyes. Perhaps a diary written by Shabanu? How does she view the concept of freedom, her own freedom within the culture?
• Who is Shabanu? Construct a family tree.
• Where does she live? Make models of the house.
• Describe her daily life.
• What are her responsibilities?
• What are her expectations in life?
• What does she value?
• What are her treasured objects?
• How does she find joy in her life?

A* Compare how Shabanu finds joy at the beginning with how she finds it at the end of the novel. How has Shabanu changed?

A* Create a double Venn Diagram to show how the similarities and differences between four characters of the same culture can bring to light cultural norms, usually in the "similarity" area but often in the "individual" areas. See the grade seven student-made diagrams which follow.

A* Create a character sociogram. By isolating, in a few words, the predominant nature of the relationships between characters, students discover cultural and social expectations.

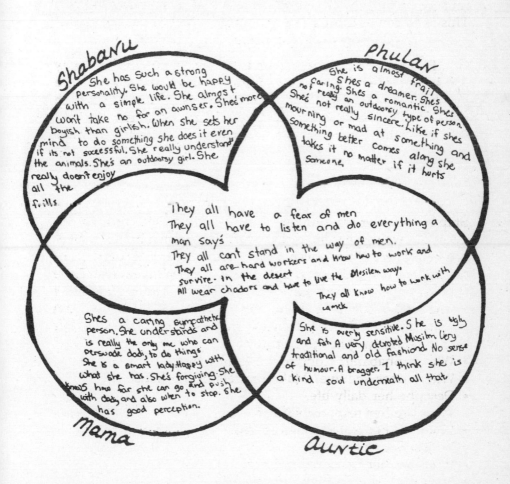

Shabanu

She has such a strong personality. She would be happy with a simple life. She almost won't take no for an awnser. She's more boyish than girlish. When she sets her mind to do something she does it even if its not successful. She really understands the animals. She's an outdoorsy girl. She really doesn't enjoy all the frills.

Phulan

She is almost frail no caring. She's a dreamer. She's not really an outdoorsy type of person. She's not really sincere. Like if she's mourning or mad at something and something better comes along she takes it no matter if it hurts someone.

They all have a fear of men
They all have to listen and do everything a man says
They all cant stand in the way of men.
They all are hard workers and know how to work and survive. In the desert
All wear chadors and have to live the Moslem way.
They all know how to work with camel.

Mama

She's a caring sympathetic person. She understands and is really the only one who can persuade dadi, to do things. She is a smart lady. Happy with what she has. She's forgiving. She knows how far she can go, and push with dadi and also when to stop. She has good perception.

Auntie

She is overly sensitive. She is ugly and fat. A very devoted Muslim. Very traditional and old fashioned. No sense of humour. A bragger. I think she is a kind soul underneath all that.

Shabanu
daughter of the wind

Shabanu
- wild as the wind
- didn't obey without fighting
- loved to care for the animals (camels)
- argued with the choices her parents made
- was close to her father
- had the wits to face other men and say witty things to them
- while at the market she was a real bargainer (in sibi)
- very friendly

Phulan
- acted very mature at a semi young age
- obeyed and didn't fight with anything her parents said
- at one point (when Hamir died) Phulan was said to marry Murad, Phulan seemed to adjust to the change easily, for getting about Shabanu's life
- demanding (at marriage time)

- after marriage had to submit their lives to their husband
- hopes to have boys
- had to obey men and weren't able to go far, in the desert were able to show faces, but in town couldn't show their faces
- had to prepare meals

Mama
- gentle
- didn't expect much
- internetized Auntie's degra remarks
- afraid for Shabanu because Shabanu disobeyed
- made sure her daughters would have good marriage or encouraged them that it was going to be alright
- obeyed well, did not talk back

Auntie
- grumpy
- didn't care for the girls very much
- boasted about herself for having boys and Mama having girls
- wasn't easy to talk to
- sometimes she thought she could do things but they backfired on her (nose ring for the camel)

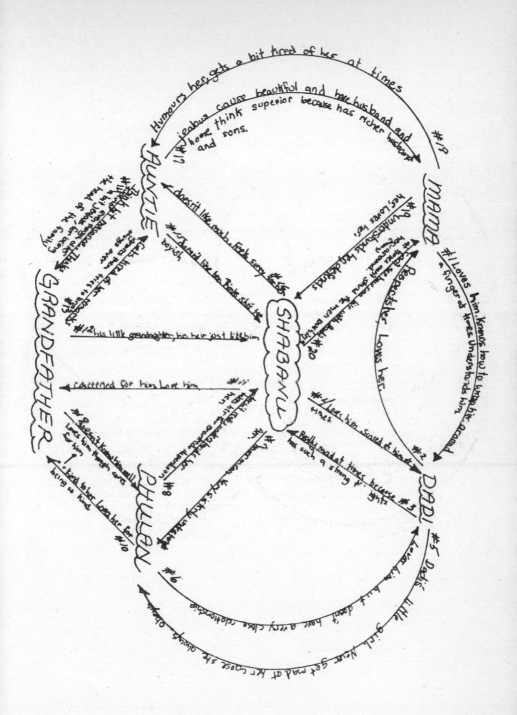

119

Camels play a significant role in the culture of these nomads, as camels are obviously their main livelihood. The camel is the ever-present "ship of the desert" in the novel.

A* Transition art: encourage students to visualize the metaphor "camels as the ships of the desert." A student example follows.

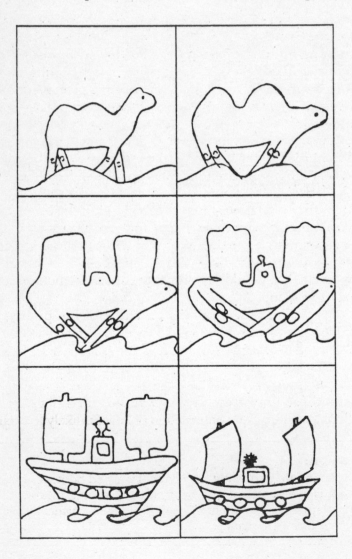

What do you know about camels? They are crucial to the lives of the people in the novel, yet what is it like to raise them?

A* Encourage students to make a chart of camel facts, listing information they have found out about camels.

DIFFICULT ISSUES

The harsh realities of desert life are dealt with matter-of-factly in this book. Events such as a miscarriage, an attempted rape, and a beating are tersely described. Student responses sometimes indicate that a serious discussion must be undertaken regarding the issues of freedom and gender as portrayed in this book. Otherwise students may come away with only negative impressions of desert life.

According to teacher Nancy Fargey, "Young readers of *Shabanu* should be guided to see the multi-faceted nature of culture/conflict issues. Perhaps a place to start to open such a conversation would be a discussion about Shabanu's father. Because the ending of this story is so honest in its description of the brutal beating of Shabanu by her father, many readers will close the book hating his actions, seeing the 'black and white' picture screened against their own cultural backdrop. I believe it is their right to hate his action, but would urge them to consider whether or not they hate the man.

"Perhaps, when they recall his purchase of the puppy, his praise for Shabanu when she saved the camel calf, his determination to bury his father according to his last wishes, and his 'guarding the backs' of the family as they fled to safety, students will discover grey areas in the debate.

"Unless these grey areas are recognized, little debate, self-evaluation, learning, or reconfirmation of belief is likely to occur."

Reflection:
One's values are frequently the result of learned heritage. Inner strength is the source of one's courage to face the future.

What happens when an immigrant brings the "justice" of his former culture to Canada?

Year of Impossible Goodbyes
Sook Nyul Choi

THE STORY

During World War II a ten-year-old Korean girl, Sookan, and her family suffer the cruelties of the long Japanese occupation of Korea. Through the eyes of this young girl, we come to know the kind strength of her grandfather and the determination of her mother, who runs a small factory making socks for the soldiers. After her grandfather dies, life changes for Sookan as she must go to a Japanese school. With the defeat of Japanese forces in 1945, the family rejoices in their freedom yet faces the reality of the country's takeover by Communist Russian troops. They believe their only hope is to flee south over the 45th parallel border to American-controlled South Korea.

FOOD FOR THOUGHT

- How do people create happiness in times of turmoil?
- How are people able to keep their spirits up in adverse conditions?
- What treasures and family heirlooms are the ones to be cherished the most?
- What do they represent?
- What cultural objects do we all keep secretly hidden away?

CAUGHT IN FROZEN IMAGES (THE SECRET TECHNIQUE!)

We can all remember moments in our lives when everything seemed to be happening in slow motion. Perhaps we had a fall, knocked something over that broke, were involved in a car accident or simply met somebody new. Time and again we replay these scenes in our minds, at liberty to create "frozen images" when needed.

This is the secret technique used by successful storytellers, public speakers, and ministers. A story or speech is divided into significant sections which can be easily visualized. The tellers then describe and elaborate on the scene as they move from image to image. This is very much like constructing a storyboard for a movie or television show.

Sook Nyul Choi is a very descriptive writer and assists readers in creating images in their minds. Read the first page of the novel aloud to the students and encourage them to quickly sketch a visual interpretation of the scene.

Choi's use of language, rich in metaphor, color, and sound (onomatopoeia), assists in creating this special sense of place throughout the story. It should also be remembered that a part of place is the mood that place creates. What are the emotions and feelings that Choi evokes in her writing?

A* Students should be encouraged to construct storyboards of the major incidents in the story. As they have to limit the number of frames in their storyboards, they are challenged to think about which incidents are necessary to tell the story. Afterwards they can compare their boards. Which incidents did they include and why?

A* Encourage students, in groups, to select one of the major incidents of the story and then form a living tableau of the scene. As they do this, enter the tableau and tap students individually on the shoulder to make them come to life. They explain in character what they are doing in the scene and what their feelings are. An exciting aspect of this activity is that things not included in the book's storytelling will be said by the students. This adds to the vitality of the telling and reflects how students' own prior experience influences what they bring to, and take from, the story. The debriefing necessary after such a session will also provide interesting insights for the students.

IMPOSSIBLE IMAGES

In any war story the writer must come to grips with the enemy. How are the occupiers personified? In this novel Choi gives us several portraits of individuals which in themselves comprise a montage of the enemy.

A* Have students make artistic representations of these images. Contrast them to those that Japanese students would draw of the Koreans. In a split screen view compare Sookan's view vs. Mrs. Narita's view of the ''Americans.''

Sookan shares her multi-faceted observations of her world. How does she perceive Captain Narita? Her Japanese schoolteacher?

A* Students can depict how Sookan's impression of the Russian soldiers comes to change from one of liberators to one of the enemy. A student example is included here.

A* Scenes between Sookan's mother and Captain Narita are especially dramatic ones for readers' theatre. The conflict between the oppressed and oppressor could be highlighted through a dramatic interpretation.

A* Invite students to examine the auditory cues associated with the enemy in this novel. They could devise a sound list with examples such as the following:

"We stood listening to the sound of their swords clanking against their guns as they walked away." (p. 53)

"Captain Narita eyed all the brassware and with his sword swept everything to the ground. The brass dishes, chopsticks and soup spoon clanked against each other as they went tumbling." (p. 26)

"Their swords and guns clanked against their belts in an all-too-familiar rhythm as they strutted past me." (p. 7)

How do these auditory images help the reader to envision the coldness of the Japanese soldiers?

Later, when the Russians take over North Korea, the narrator speaks of repeated announcements over loudspeakers, praising Communism and the Party.

"Incessantly, the loudspeaker blared the praises of the great Russian leaders. The town was so noisy I could hardly think." (p. 110)

The Russian attempts to brainwash the Koreans make Sookan realize that even though they may not be as frightening as the Japanese, they are still the enemy.

A* Students might put together a tape, "Sounds of the Enemy," or use sound effects as part of a short dramatic interpretation showing the conflict. During times of adversity, particularly war, people tend to value the cultural heritage in their lives which brings them a sense of continuity and hope. Have students identify which objects, remembrances, sights, and smells Sookan has during the occupations. What does she take as she crosses the barbed-wire fence at the border? Exhausted, with only the clothes on her back, she nonetheless carries a rich heritage with her. Combining words and pictures will help students to create a collage of cultural images describing the heritage Sookan carries with her.

IMPOSSIBLE GOODBYES

This writer has very powerfully integrated her title throughout the novel as the young girl must say goodbye to a series of images, objects, people and places—the list is a long one.

Encourage your students to compile a list of the things that Sookan has to say goodbye to. After the search for Sookan's goodbyes, encourage the students to share the important goodbyes they have experienced in their lives. This may be especially poignant if a student has recently immigrated. If not, ask the students what they think it would be like if they were to go to live in another country. What would they have to leave behind and say goodbye to? What if they had to leave our planet due to environmental damage? What would they take?

A* Encourage your students to think about characters in other books they have read and to share the goodbyes they had to say.

Teachers should be aware that when the girls in the sock factory are taken by the troops to the front lines, they are being forced into prostitution. All reports are that the real girls received brutal treatment and most died. In 1992 the Japanese prime minister, Mr. Kiichi Miyazawa, apologized for "the suffering and sorrow" caused by his country.

Reflection:
The images associated with the portrayal of the Japanese in this book may be found too unnerving and frightening, too real. Will this perpetuate a hatred of the Japanese? Teachers need to be prepared to discuss this issue and have alternative images ready. The real issue is of mass brutality of any kind—why? to whom?

Cultural Voices in Translation

It is important for Canadian students to be aware of writers and illustrators from other countries. They need to recognize their names, their works, and the fact that they are writing about the lives of youngsters very much like themselves. There is a little bit of Pippi Longstocking, Tin Tin, or Heidi in each one of us. We just need to recognize it and appreciate it.

Translations form a major part of our western literary heritage. What would our lives and those of our students in the English-speaking world be like without great pieces of literature such as the following:

	(date of translation)
The Arabian Nights	1712
Swiss Family Robinson	1814
Grimm's Household Stories	1823
Andersen's Fairy Tales	1846
Around the World in 80 Days	1872
Heidi	1884
Pinocchio	1891
Bambi	1929

The tradition of translating literature for young people is a long-standing one in Europe. Surrounded by many languages, people accept its necessity as part of their daily way of life. Between 30 and 70 per cent of the children's books published on that continent are translated.

A major issue here is inferior translations. Professional translators are crucial if text quality, cultural honesty, and the rights of young readers are to be respected. Translators of literature require an appreciation of and insight into the schema of literature, the importance of literary devices such as simile and metaphor, as well as a respect for the structure of the story. The translation of fiction for young people is exceptionally demanding because it requires the translator to transpose the work into a second language as if the writer were also writing in it, yet always consider the danger of distancing the young audience from the story. There is more than just direct translation of words—culture, customs, and current expressions must also be considered.

All children need to have the opportunity to read the best literature from other countries so as to increase their international understanding. A partial list follows.

TRANSLATED LITERATURE FOR CHILDREN

9+   *Conrad* by Christine Nöstlinger (German)
      Sunday's Child by Gurun Mebs (German)

10+   *The Island on Bird Street* by Uri Orlev (Hebrew)
      Offbeat Friends by Elfie Donnelly (German)

11+   *Boris* by Jaap ter Haar (Dutch)
      Fly Away Home by Christine Nöstlinger (German)
      Friedrich by Hans Peter Richter (German)
      I Am David by Anne Holm (Danish)
      Paper Bird by Maretha Maartens (Afrikaans)
      Petros' War by Alki Zei (Greek)
      Buster's World by Bjarne Reuter (Danish)

12+   *The Man from the Other Side* by Uri Orlev (Hebrew)
      Along the Tracks by Tamar Bergman (Hebrew)
      Crutches by Peter Härtling (German)
      Shadows across the Sun by Albert Likhanov (Russian)
      Becoming Gershona by Nava Semel (Hebrew)

Young Adult

Many titles in translation are appropriate for more mature readers. Each offers a rich insight into a culture as viewed through the eyes of a teenager. Recommended titles include:

I Was There by Hans Peter Richter. Translated from the German by Edite Kroll.

A Hand Full of Stars by Rafik Schami. Translated from the German by Rika Lesser.

MILDRED L. BATCHELDER AWARD

Since 1968 this annual award has been given by the American Library Association to the American publisher of a children's book considered to be the most outstanding of those published first abroad in a foreign language and later in the United States. Any title on the list, which you can obtain easily from your library or the ALA, is worth looking at.

THE HANS CHRISTIAN ANDERSEN AWARD

The International Board on Books for Young People (IBBY) gives this award every two years in recognition of an outstanding contribution to the writing and illustration of books for children. The list of winners is a virtual who's who of excellent literature from cultures around the world, and well worth looking at.

Cultural Visions

"Show me!"

Students today are more visually conscious than ever because of the impact of television and videos. Thus, the sharing of another culture is often stronger and more engaging if it is done in a visual format. Students can be challenged to discover and learn about the many talented artists in the world who now find satisfying artistic challenges in creating picture books. Picture books for older readers have become an important part of multicultural literature.

Consideration, therefore, should be given to the picture book as an artistic entity. The cover, jacket, flyleaf, and title page of the book are all worthy of study. What is the importance and impact of the color choice? Is there a change in the tonal quality as the story develops? Is there a sense of an artistic motif throughout the book? Have certain symbols been integrated throughout it?

Picture books offer powerful insights into cultures through images of different settings, activities, and customs.

Identify the cultural elements which are present in specific books. Which ones make the culture appear unique and real?

Three types of books provide rich visual images of culture. These are appropriate for all ages.

1. FOLKTALES

Many multicultural book lists are filled with folktales, each elaborately illustrated with the arts and crafts of the original culture. This is all well and good, depending on the accuracy of the artistic interpretation, but unless folktales are given special attention to indicate their relevance for children today, they will be viewed only as examples of past glory bearing little relevance to the present. Comments related to the sharing of these tales and recommended editions can found in chapter 2.

2. PHOTOGRAPHIC ESSAYS

Books such as these often highlight children sharing daily routines and activities in their lives. The photographs may be of a higher quality than the text because frequently the text is written mainly to accommodate the photos. It is actually the photos accompanied by their captions that provide youngsters with a glimpse into another culture. Carolrhoda publishes a "Children of ..." series that features such countries as China, Egypt, and Nepal. Lerner Publishers have two remarkable titles, *Children of Clay; A Family of Pueblo Potters* by Rina Swentzell, and *The Sacred Harvest; Ojibway Wild Rice Gathering* by Gordon Regguinti.

3. CULTURAL INTERPRETATIONS

These books feature illustrations that sensitively and accurately highlight a distinctive cultural environment or happenings in the lives of young people. They may be realistic or fanciful in nature.

A good example of the genre is Cynthia Rylant's *Appalachia: The Voices of Sleeping Birds*, illustrated by Barry Moser. Reminiscent glimpses of a remembered region; the people, the place, the dogs. Poetic language evokes the flavor of relaxed memories.

Watercolor images appear frozen in time. The tone of each illustration reflects the quiet morning in the region rather than a cultural portrait of it, yet each is strangely moving and filled with anticipation.

Margaret Musgrove's *Ashanti to Zulu; African Traditions*, with pictures by Leo and Diane Dillon, is an alphabet book with such an unexpected, changing flavor that it serves as an introduction to a variety of peoples and their customs from the big continent.

Rich, opulent illustrations reflect the reality that Africa is not one culture but many diverse ones, each distinctive in its own right. Each letter of the alphabet features a tribal group and some aspect of their culture. An elegantly clad Ewe drummer "talks" with his ornately decorated drum, Masai men take special care with their hair, using red clay and cow grease to highlight the multitude of tiny braids; and a Ouadai market is resplendent with bright print cloths and vegetable products. The extensive research of the illustrators is evident in the details within each scene.

Chapter 5

Cultural Cross-Checks

The question lurks at the back of every reader's mind. As adults we are sometimes too shy to ask, but students are not and frequently do when given the opportunity. In a good story, characters seem so real, situations so probable, and cultural setting so convincing that we as readers enter into the author's world willingly and believingly.

When reading or sharing cultural literary experiences, we as teachers and librarians need to be conscious of the accuracy of the cultural portrait being shared. What evidence do we have that it is an honest portrait? How well does the writer or illustrator know the subject? Are they members of the cultural group depicted?

Why is this important? Books for young people with a strong cultural sensitivity give us a greater awareness of the elements of culture and insights into specific aspects of a culture that we may have been unaware of.

The sharing process allows a special pride to develop in individuals of the culture being examined, as they may discover new details and customs of their heritage, a sense of their own history, and a pride in their identity.

In what ways can we as individual readers find out about the authenticity of a cultural portrait? Firstly, consult reviews in leading review journals such as *Kirkus, Booklist*, and *Horn Book*. Secondly, locate relevant articles and books which are explanations by the writers themselves or which are critical assessments. *Booklinks*, published by the American Library Association, is a good resource for this. Thirdly, make personal contact with writers, illustrators, and publishers. The best method is to actually invite writers or illustrators to your school or library. These individuals are only too glad to share with readers their hours of research to heighten the accuracy of their books. Another way to meet writers or illustrators is to attend meetings of your local Children's Literature Roundtable where they are speaking. You could also go to a large conference, such as those of the American Library Association, the IRA, or the NCTE, where they are featured.

Conducting a Cultural Cross-Check

To assess the validity of the cultural portrait in a book, evidence should be available which indicates the experience, resources, and expert consultations used in the process. Be certain to check inside the jacket flap or the book itself for notes or sources of further information. The following four major areas should be considered.

1. EXPERTISE OF THE WRITER OR ILLUSTRATOR

Whether the writer and illustrator are members of the cultural group or not, an accurate portrait of a culture can only be made by an individual who is knowledgeable, has had extensive experience with the culture, and is a keen observer of people and places.

Suzanne Fisher Staples, for instance, author of *Shabanu, Daughter of the Wind*, was the correspondent for United Press International (UPI) in Asia for twelve years. She lived in Pakistan for three years, and during this time she developed a keen interest in the people of the desert, particularly the women.

During talks she has given, Ms. Staples has shared how she lived with them for extended periods. She dressed in similar clothes, spoke their language (Urdu), practiced their religion, ate with them, pulled water out of deep wells, and walked in the desert with them. She wanted to get as close to their experience as possible—to sense the rope biting into her hand, the sand burning through her sandals and a sandstorm stinging like needles on her face. In the evening, sitting around the fire, the women shared stories, talked of their dreams, and told of events affecting girls which eventually found their way into her book. She wanted to show that although the veil is a symbol of oppression and the inferiority of women in this culture, it is also their identity—not something to hide behind or to be used as a shield. She notes that it is not Islam that oppresses but rather poverty and ignorance. She feels that only through a thorough understanding of differences and similarities can we truly understand others.

Ian Wallace's first memories of the dragon dances at New Year's celebrations resulted in *Chin Chiang and the Dragon's Dance*. He was so excited by his experience that he decided to tell the story of the dance, a tradition of movements handed down from one generation to another. He did tell the story, but it took him six long years. He did extensive research in the reference library of the Toronto Public Library and consulted with an expert in East Asian Studies at the University of Toronto. He also visited Vancouver for research at the Chinese Cultural Centre and for onsite sketching of the buildings and people he would use in the illustrations. He even included his landlords as characters. Some concern was expressed afterwards about the fact that an old woman took part in the Dragon dance. Authorities, however, will tell you that the New Year's Dragon dance was traditionally a people's dance and open to anyone in the community—anyone, that is, who could hold up the pole under the heavy beast. In larger centres the emphasis has changed and now martial arts groups have taken it over. It is a matter of interpretation; we all celebrate Christmas in a variety of ways (all being the "correct" way!), so too is New Year's celebrated in similar but differing ways.

2. EVIDENCE OF RESEARCH UNDERTAKEN

Many writers and illustrators include references to where they did research, each giving credit to museum staff members, experts, listing relevant resources.

Illustrators frequently use the collections of such museums as the Royal Ontario Museum, UBC's Museum of Anthropology, and Ottawa's Museum of Civilization to examine artifacts and objects. This is of particular significance to achieve the exact texture, pattern, design, and color of specific objects.

Elizabeth Cleaver was an illustrator who at times asked friends to assist in her research. I still remember her asking me to go to Sarospatak's castle of Rakoczy in Eastern Hungary to take pictures of the tiles behind the large stoves. She wanted to make certain that her sketches for *The Miraculous Hind* were accurate and that her memory, based on a previous trip, served her correctly.

Brenda Clark illustrated *Little Fingerling*, a Japanese folktale retold by Monica Hughes. It proved to be a great challenge for Brenda as she stated in a press release, "I learned so much when I did this book. It gave me an opportunity to do research about Japanese history and art." She notes that she did not want to copy Japanese style precisely. "If I had strictly followed the Japanese woodcut style, the characters wouldn't have had any expression. So in this book they're semi-stylized, but with expression. I wanted the faces to have personality."

Brenda did extensive research for her illustrations. Initially, she spent time in bookstores locating editions of Japanese folktales to ascertain what was available and to compare them. Then she went to the Toronto Public Library's picture library to study their collection. Finally, for four months, before even the first illustration was done, she went daily to the Royal Ontario Museum's Far East collections and studied the artifacts, made extensive use of the museum's library, and consulted with two experts. She was permitted to see artifacts that were not on public display. After the first rough illustrations were done, she again returned to the museum's experts and had them check them.

Paul Morin is an example of an illustrator who goes to the site to conduct research for his illustrations. He actually mortgaged his home in order to take a trip to Kenya to do research for Tololwa M. Mollel's *The Orphan Boy*. He spent two months there living with a Masai tribe. He was befriended by a young warrior and thus was able to experience life as he lived it. This trip enabled him to include his friends as characters in the book, at the same time adding authenticity to the interpretation. Paul is unusual in another way; he brings back materials to add to his paintings to enrich them and give them a new depth. He uses straw, dirt, and sand that he picked up in Kenya for his view of the Serengetti.

Paul went to Yangshuo in China to research images for the setting and the characters in *The Dragon's Pearl*, written by Julie Lawson. While in China he bargained for an ancient Chinese coin and put it into an illustration. He takes many slides so that he can view them when he returns to his Ontario studio.

The link between picture books for young people and museum collections should be fully realized by educators and museum curators. It is, in fact, a source of surprise and delight to students as they go armed with relevant cultural picture books to their local museum to become "artifact finders" trying to find the real thing.

A* I like to encourage students to become cultural sleuths. Is it authentic? Is the pattern real? Find it! Build a case for your book based on real artifacts. Working in pairs or trios is always more fun as the excited chatter accompanying a find will tell the listening teacher. The important thing is not how many artifacts students find, but rather the links being made between illustration, text, and artifact. The students are using a method much like that an illustrator would use prior to creating a book.

We in Vancouver are fortunate to have the remarkable Museum of Anthropology at the University of British Columbia. Besides the main display areas, there is an active research collection consisting of drawers and showcases brimming with ethnological treasures.

What can be found in an expedition to such a place? In the African section, various artifacts can be seen. Examining Verna Aardema's *Bringing the Rain to Kapiti Plain* students might find a lyre-type string instrument similar to ones found in the Upper Nile region, or a spear of the hero might be seen in Zambia. Items that could have belonged to Ki-pat's family are an upper arm bracelet, jewelry, a stool, and various types of pottery with appropriate designs.

The exhibits reveal many items evidenced in Ann Grifalconi's *Village of Round and Square Houses*. These include bracelets similar to those worn by the child early in the story, numerous hut models, examples of clay cooking pots with handles, and pipes similar to the one smoked by Grandma, as well as many types of baskets. If you are near a museum, find out whether its collection can add to what you and your students are reading.

A* No museum readily available? The same kind of exploration can be undertaken by using resources from your local public library. Arrange to borrow several adult art and ethnographic references and have the students scour the pages searching for objects, patterns, and designs which resemble those in a story they are reading. The commentary given by experts will further enhance and extend their aesthetic awareness of the cultural objects of other peoples. This research can also be done by groups who have actually seen the objects, as it will reinforce and extend their artistic awareness and appreciation.

A* Personal museums. Based on the concept of "artifact finders," students could be encouraged to design and make museums in their own classroom or in the school library resource centre. They could go from the picture book to the adult reference to real objects and then construct a three-dimensional representation. Most important is the wording of the explanatory card that should accompany each object. In this one activity many subject areas can be integrated.

4. CULTURAL CROSS-CHECKS

One effective means of cross-checking is to share a book with a person from the cultural group featured in it and ask them to talk about any aspects of their culture they notice. Ask neighbors, parents, fellow workers, teachers, librarians, and friends to assist you. An important point is that one must keep in mind the cultural awareness of each individual. How qualified are they to know about the details of their culture? What experiences have they had? One thing that needs to be considered is whether the person was born in their culture's homeland or in Canada. A good example is that the views of an Issei (born in Japan) may be different from a Nisei (first generation born in Canada), a Sensi (second generation), or a Sansei (third generation). The distance in time a person is removed from the home culture may have some bearing on their knowledge and views.

In the case of *Little Fingerling* by Monica Hughes, illustrated by Brenda Clark, I asked five individuals to give me their comments. Immediately, they noted that the book is set in the Edo period of Japanese history (1603-1868), a time just before the opening of the country to westerners, hence in a traditional period. The women's hairstyles were a major indicator as the upswept coiffure is distinctive of this period.

All of the individuals were impressed with the accuracy of the details in the illustrations, evidence of much research on the part of the artist.

For several readers, however, the color of the illustrations in this book was not felt to be Japanese—the blues were too clear and too transparent, lacking depth and richness. When I asked Brenda Clark about this comment, she noted that she was not using the traditional wood-block technique with inks, but watercolors. This was the reason the illustrations were more vivid than Japanese prints, the ink in which gives a darker and richer tone.

The contrast in scenes between that of the interior of a peasant's hut and that of a nobleman's house illustrates the class structure in Japan. Clark received rave reviews for her authentic representation of details in the settings. The farmer's house was simplicity in the extreme, every artifact with a practical purpose—the roughly carved wooden table, the rice tatami mats on the floor, the bamboo whisk in the ash sill, the wooden comb in the mother's hair, the handmade water bucket. The only concern readers had was whether Issun Boshi would actually help his mother, as Japanese boys traditionally do not.

Reinforcement like this of a book's accuracy from members of the culture described is invaluable. You might even want to invite your "verifiers" to talk to your class.

REVIEWS: CULTURAL CONSIDERATIONS

Rarely do reviews of children's books comment on the accuracy of either the written or artistic interpretation of a culture. Reviewers have a tendency to focus on the literary aspects, those devoid of any cultural implication. This is done obviously in the belief that all books of quality must tell a good story. There is also a reluctance to take on the authenticity question. Authentic in whose eyes? This is a major question of interpretation. Are members of the culture reviewing the books?

When a review does question the creator of a book, it is reassuring to know that editors of such reviewing journals as *School Library Journal* allow dialogue. This recently occurred and the following is the resulting exchange. Such debate is healthy, and often revealing for readers.

BROTHER EAGLE, SISTER SKY. illus. by Susan Jeffers. Unpaged. CIP. Dial. Sept. 1991. Tr $14.95. ISBN 0-8037-0969-2; PLB $14.89. ISBN 0-8037-0963-3. LC 90-27713.

Gr 1-5—Chief Sealth (called "Seattle" by Jeffers) may not, in fact, be the historical source of the speech commonly attributed to him, and abridged and adapted here. But the message it conveys has never been more pointed, poignant, and powerful, Jeffers's popular pen-and-color style means that the illustrations are romantic and attractive. Alas, her entire stock of characters appears to have come from Sioux Central Casting, complete with Plains ponies and tipis (and one incongruous birchbark canoe lifted from the Algonquians). The beautiful and important words of the text ("The earth does not belong to us. We belong to the earth... All things are connected like the blood that unites us.") are not well served by images that ignore the rich diversity of Amerindian cultures (even Sealth's own Northwest people) in favor of cigar-store redskins in feathers and fringe. Where Jeffers's book is used, it should be supplemented with others more sensitive to Native American heritage.—*Patricia Dooley, University of Washington, Seattle*

School Library Journal, September 1991 (V.37, No.9), p. 228

BROTHER EAGLE, SISTER SKY

I am very glad that your reviewer found *Brother Eagle, Sister Sky* (Dial, 1991; Sept., p. 228) "poignant and powerful." I took on the challenge of creating this book because children need to know that the Earth and every creature on it are sacred. My illustrations may be limited by my artistic and scholarly abilities but not by a lack of desire to give a magnificent philosophy its due.

Dooley states that neither Chief Seattle's own people nor the diverse cultures of other Native American groups are represented. The tribesmen and dugout canoe on the title page are of the Northwest Coastal nations of which Seattle was a chief. Throughout the book I portrayed peoples and artifacts from a wide array of nations: Cheyenne, Chippewa, Nez Perce, Lokota, Black Foot as well as Northern Algonquian, who were pictured with the birchbark canoe. Your reviewer called the canoe "incongruous," apparently because she thought I had painted only Sioux throughout the book. I represented as broad a range of cultures as I could within the scope of the picture book format. I included them because the philosophy expressed in the text is one shared by all Native American groups, as I point out on the last page.

My research for the book was extensive. I spent much time in the museums of the American Indian and Natural History in New York and The Victoria Museum and the Museum on Quadra Island in British Columbia, among others. I also visited reservations in the Northwest and Southwest. Among my references were Curtis and Catlin pictures and diaries as well as actual shirts, leggings, canoes, cradleboards, dresses, moccasins, and artifacts preserved in the museums and worn at festivals and pow wows. Mag La Que, Miyaca, Mahto-Topah and Bear Woman—all Lakota Sioux—edited the text and drawings and sat for portraits.

Dooley speaks of "cigar-store redskins in feathers and fringe." In a recent issue of *Smithsonian Magazine*, there is a reproduction of Kicking Bear's own drawing of the Battle of Little Bighorn, in which he took part. The drawing shows chiefs and warriors garbed in buckskin, fringe, and feathers.

The movement to repair and protect our Earth is not just a trendy issue; it is a legacy of a culture older and sometimes wiser than our own. I am concerned that concentrating on the spelling of Chief Seattle's name and the clothing of the Indians may cause readers (of this review) to miss the point of the book. My hope in creating it was that it might help us learn from the exemplary relationship Native Americans had with the Earth—for the benefit of all our children.

SUSAN JEFFERS
Croton On Hudson, NY

OUR REVIEWER REPLIES:

It is precisely because the movement Ms. Jeffers supports is *not* trendy but the worthwhile legacy of a real culture that I expect her to spell its spokesman's name right.

As for the representation of Northwest Coast peoples: I do not find the "tribesmen" she cites on the title page on my copy of *Brother Eagle, Sister Sky*. In the distance, past several eagles five times larger, is a dugout canoe and a single figure, exactly one inch high. A magnifying lens might help confirm (his? her?) Northwest origins. Readers are, I fear, understandably likely to assume that the large, impressively bonneted face dominating the dust jacket belongs to "Chief Seattle," in the absence of other candidates.

The "wide array of nations" Ms. Jeffers lists in her letter are all either Great Plains or Great Lakes peoples. Ms. Jeffers herself identifies the editors and models she names as Sioux—just as the review said. I do not question the research the illustrator did, or the authenticity of the artifacts and dress she chose to depict. My objection is that these images conform to a "type," or stock figure, already fixed in popular culture; indeed, the *only* image attached to the word "Indian" for many children.

It is the message in Sealth's speech that I praised as "poignant and powerful,'' and I share Jeffers's hope for the spread of that message.

PATRICIA DOOLEY
Mercer Island, WA

Teachers must become aware of the importance of a sensitive and accurate cultural portrait in both illustration and text if an attitude of respect for the culture of others is to be achieved. Consider the following final factors as a selection guide.

1. Respect for a Culture

- Is the culture presented with a sense of respect?
- What evidence do we have that the culture of the characters is accurately presented?
- Is the experience shared in the story one which would be authentic for the culture?
- Do descriptive words or artistic details indicate a realistic/true image of the culture?

2. Avoidance of Stereotypes

- Are individuals portrayed as being unique regardless of culture?
- Is a diversity of physical and psychological traits presented?

3. Literary Structure

- Are the settings accurate for the time and place?
- Is the story based on correct information (historical or recent)?
- If dialect is used, does it seem real and become a natural part of the story?

Conclusion

The ideas for experiencing literature and culture presented in this book are intended to be a starting point for many directions of exploration and reflection. If we believe that good children's books help to make for a better world, then we will continue to make the best literature available to our youngsters. Only by being able to walk in a character's shoes and experience insights into another culture will we be able to realize true international understanding.

The recommended titles are to some extent personal choices, reflecting my experiences and beliefs but also the views found in reviews and the opinions of colleagues in the field of children's literature in many parts of the world. In many countries publishers are heeding the demand of educators, and more and more cultural stories are being published.

We should consider the following statement from IBBY, the International Board on Books for Young People.

> Assuming that the world of the future will be shaped by the minds and hands of our children, surely we want these children to be equipped with their ideas and ideals, the information and inspiration they need in order to make of it a better place. Our concern must reach beyond their physical material well-being to include their physical, psychological and cultural development. In these children is the whole potentiality of the human race....
>
> In books they can find the records of humanity's achievements of the past and the tools for achieving its aspirations for the future. Let us give children the books they need today for a better world tomorrow. Books to promote friendship, peace and understanding: books that introduce people who have other ways of living; books that present a

variety of ethnic groups and cultures in a positive and non-stereotyped manner; books that prepare children for living harmoniously in an interdependent world; books to tell them of their own ethnic heritage... Books that, while recognizing the value of cultural differences, yet emphasize the many things shared by all of humankind... Books that foster concern for the earth, the single small planet on which we all live together....

Reflection:

Early on in this book I mentioned the questions I like to ask the teachers in my multicultural children's literature course; now is the time for you to reflect on them again.

- What universal constants among cultures are portrayed in children's books?
- In what ways are children's books a reflection of the society in which they were written?
- What benefits are gained by children when they read cross-cultural literature?
- What is the importance to the self-concept of children in being able to recognize themselves in cross-cultural literature?
- How can the authenticity of a culture portrayed in literature for children be assessed?
- Do countries have literary mosaics? What is the image of Canada (or any country/culture) in children's books? Which books could help recent immigrants to learn about Canada and its people?
- What is the relevance of the comment made by Janet Lunn, "No country is ever settled just once. Each new generation must settle it again in their imaginations"?
- Why is it important for educators to go beyond the traditional "F" approach to multiculturalism (Food, Festivals, Folklore, Fun), and how can literature enrich multicultural understanding and experience?

Bibliography

This bibliography of culturally oriented books for intermediate readers is arranged by genre. You and your students will make many serendipitous discoveries by sharing a wide range of these titles, rather than focusing exclusively on one cultural group. Only those titles which are considered to have outstanding qualities as cultural experiences are included. Of course, the list is not comprehensive; you will discover many more on your own. Where applicable, the paperback publisher has been listed, so you can get the latest, most inexpensive edition.

Fiction

Arlington, Gabriel. *The Stars Are Upside Down*. Heinemann, 1990.

Bell, William. *Absolutely Invincible*. Stoddart, 1991.

Bell, William. *Forbidden City*. Stoddart, 1991.

Bell, William. *No Signature*. Doubleday, 1992.

Berry, James. *Ajeemah and His Son*. HarperCollins, 1992.

Buss, Fran Leeper. *Journey of the Sparrows*, written with the assistance of Daisy Cubias. Lodestar, 1991.

Cameron, Ann. *The Most Beautiful Place in the World*. Drawings by Bullseye, 1993.

Case, Dianne. *Love, David*. Lodestar, 1991.

Castañeda, Omar S. *Among the Volcanoes*. Lodestar, 1991.

Choi, Sook Nyul. *Year of Impossible Goodbyes*. Dell, 1993.

Cleary, Beverly. *Dear Mr. Henshaw*. Dell, 1992.

Coerr, Eleanor. *Sadako and the Thousand Paper Cranes*. Paintings by Ronald Himler. Dell, 1979.

Collier, James and Christopher. *Jump Ship to Freedom*. Delacorte, 1981.

Collura, Mary-Ellen Lang. *Winners*. Western Producer Prairie Books/Douglas & McIntyre, 1984.

Desai, Anita. *The Village by the Sea*. Puffin, 1984.

Donnelly, Elfie. *Offbeat Friends*. Translated from the German by Anthea Bell. Crown, 1981.

Doros, Arthur. *Abuela*. Dutton, 1991.

Doyle, Brian. *Angel Square*. Groundwood, 1992.

Doyle, Brian. *Easy Avenue*. Groundwood, 1992.

Ellis, Sarah. *Next-Door Neighbours*. Groundwood, 1989.

Fenner, Carol. *Randall's Wall*. McElderry, 1991.

Fox, Paula. *Slave Dancer*. Dell, 1991.

Fritz, Jean. *Homesick: My Own Story*. Dell, 1982.

Garrigue, Sheila. *The Eternal Spring of Mr. Ito*. Bradbury, 1985.

Gavin, Jamila. *Double Dare*. Mammoth, 1992.

Gavin, Jamila. *The Singing Bowls*. Mandarin, 1990.

Gavin, Jamila. *The Wheel of Surya*. Methuen, 1992.

Gordon, Sheila. *Waiting for the Rain*. Bantam, 1989.

Graham, Gail. *Crossfire*. Pantheon, 1972.

Greenfield, Eloise. *Daydreamers*. Illustrated by Tom Feelings. Dial, 1985.

Greenfield, Eloise. *Talk about a Family*. Illlustrated by James Calvin. HarperCollins, 1991.

Guy, Roasa. *The Friends*. Bantam, 1983.

Hahn, Mary Downing. *Stepping on the Cracks*. Clarion, 1991.

Hamilton, Virginia. *Cousins*. Philomel, 1990.

Hamilton, Virginia. *The House of Dies Drear*. Illustrated by Eros Keith. Macmillan, 1968.

Hamilton, Virginia. *M.C. Higgins the Great*. Aladdin, 1993.

Hamilton, Virginia. *The Mystery of Drear House*. Greenwillow, 1987.

Hamilton, Virginia. *Zeely*. Illustrated by Symeon Shimin. Aladdin, 1993.

Härtling, Peter. *Old John*. Translated from the German by Elizabeth D. Crawford. Lothrop, Lee & Shepard, 1990.

Harvey, Brett. *Immigrant Girl: Beck of Eldridge Street*. Illustrated by Deborah K. Ray. Holiday, 1987.

Heneghan, Jim. *Promises to Come*. Overlea, 1988 (op).

Hesse, Karen. *Letters from Rifka*. Holt, 1992.

Hiçyilmaz, Gaye. *Against the Storm*. Illustrated by Mei-Yim Low. Puffin, 1991.

Horne, Constance. *Nykola and Granny*. Gage, 1989.

Houston, James. *Drifting Snow: An Arctic Search*. McClelland & Stewart, 1992.

Houston, James. *Frozen Fire*. Aladdin, 1992.

Houston, James. *Tikta'liktak*. Harcourt Brace Jovanovich, 1990.

Hughes, Monica. *Beyond the Dark River*. Stoddart, 1992.

Hughes, Monica. *Keeper of the Isis Light*. Mammoth, 1991.

Hughes, Monica. *My Name Is Paula Popowich*. Lorimer, 1983.

Hunter, Mollie. *A Stranger Came Ashore*. Harper Trophy, 1977.

Hurwitz, Johanna. *Once I Was a Plum Tree*. Beech Tree/Morrow, 1992.

Huynh, Quang Nhuong. *The Land I Lost: Adventures of a Boy in Vietman*. Harper, 1986.

Joseph, Lynn. *A Wave in Her Pocket: Stories from Trinidad*. Clarion, 1991.

Kidd, Diana. *Onion Tears*. Illustrated by Lucy Montgomery. Orchard, 1991.

Kogawa, Joy. *Naomi's Road*. Oxford, 1986.

Kraus, Joanna Halpert. *Tall Boy's Journey*. Illustrated by Karen Ritz. Carolrhoda, 1992.

Laird, Elizabeth. *Kiss the Dust*. Mammoth, 1993.

Lester, Julius. *Long Journey Home: Stories from Black History*. Dial, 1972.

Lester, Julius. *To Be a Slave*. Illustrated by Tom Feelings. Scholastic, 1986.

Lingard, Joan. *Tug of War*. Puffin, 1992.

Lingard, Joan. *The Twelfth Day of July*. (op)

Little, Jean. *Mama's Going to Buy You a Mockingbird*. Puffin, 1985.

Lord, Bette Bao. *In the Year of the Boar and Jackie Robinson*. Illustrated by Marc Simont. Harper & Row, 1984.

Loverseed, Amanda. *Tikkatou's Journey*. Danwell, 1990.

Lowry, Lois. *Number the Stars*. Dell, 1990.

Lunn, Janet. *The Root Cellar*. Puffin, 1983.

Lunn, Janet. *Shadow in Hawthorn Bay*. Puffin, 1988.

Lyons, Mary E. *Letters from a Slave Girl: The Story of Harriet Jacobs*. Scribners, 1992.

Maartens, Maretha. *Paper Bird*. Translated from the Afrikaans by Madeleine van Biljon. Clarion, 1990.

MacLachlan, Patricia. *Journey*. Delacorte, 1991.

Mahy, Margaret. *Memory*. Penguin, 1989.

Mebs, Gudrun. *Sunday's Child*. Translated from the German by Sara Gibson. Dell, 1989.

Mowat, Farley. *Lost in the Barrens*. Illustrated by Charles Geer. McClelland & Stewart, 1988.

Myers, Walter Dean. *Fallen Angels*. Scholastic, 1988.

Myers, Walter Dean. *Fast Sam, Cool Clyde & Stuff*. Puffin, 1988.

Myers, Walter Dean. *Now Is Your Time! The African-American Struggle for Freedom*. HarperCollins, 1991.

Myers, Walter Dean. *The Outside Shot*. Dell, 1984.

Myers, Walter Dean. *Scorpions*. Harper Trophy, 1990.

Myers, Walter Dean. *Won't Know Until I Get There*. Viking, 1982.

Naidoo, Beverley. *Chain of Fire*. Lippincott, 1990.

Naidoo, Beverley. *Journey to Jo'burg*. Harper Trophy, 1988.

Namioka, Lensey. *Yang the Youngest and His Terrible Ear*. Illustrated by Kees de Kiefte. Little, 1992.

Nixon, Joan Lowry. *Ellis Island, Land of Hope*. Bantam, 1992.

Paterson, Katherine. *Park's Quest*. Puffin, 1989.

Paulsen, Gary. *Dogsong*. Puffin, 1987.

Paulsen, Gary. *Nightjohn*. Delacorte, 1993.

Pearson, Kit. *The Sky Is Falling*. Penguin, 1989.

Semel, Navaa. *Becoming Gershona*. Translated from the Hebrew by Seymour Simckes. Puffin, 1992.

Smucker, Barbara. *Amish Adventure*. Puffin, 1984.

Smucker, Barbara. *Days of Terror*. Puffin, 1981.

Smucker, Barbara. *Jacob's Little Giant*. Puffin, 1988.

Smucker, Barbara. *Underground to Canada*. Penguin, 1988.

Speare, Elizabeth. *The Witch of Blackbird Pond*. Dell, 1972.

Spinelli, Jerry. *Maniac Magee*. Harper Trophy, 1992.

Spinelli, Jerry. *There's a Girl in My Hammerlock*. Little, Brown, 1992.

Staples, Suzanne Fisher. *Shabanu, Daughter of the Wind*. Sprinters, 1991.

Sterling, Shirley. *My Name Is Seepeetza*. Groundwood, 1992.

Stevens, Bryna. *Frank Thompson, Her Civil War Story*. Macmillan, 1992.

Taylor, Mildred. *The Gold Cadillac*. Illustrated by Michael Hays. Dial, 1987.

Taylor, Mildred. *Roll of Thunder, Hear My Cry*. Puffin, 1991.

Thomas, Joyce C. *The Golden Pasture*. Scholastic, 1986.

Thomas, Joyce. C. *Journey*. Scholastic, 1988.

Thomas, Joyce. C. *Marked by Fire*. Avon, 1982.

Uchida, Yoshiko. *The Best Bad Thing*. Aladdin, 1986.

Uchida, Yoshiko. *The Happiest Ending*. McElderry, 1985.

Uchida, Yoshiko. *A Jar of Dreams*. Aladdin, 1993.

Uchida, Yoshiko. *Journey Home*. Aladdin, 1992.

Uchida, Yoshiko. *Journey to Topaz*. Illustrated by Donald Carrick. Scribner, 1971.

Voigt, Cynthia. *Dicey's Song*. Fawcett Juniper, 1991.

Voigt, Cynthia. *Homecoming*. Fawcett Juniper, 1992.

Wallace, Ian, and Angela Wood. *The Sandwich*. Kids Can, 1975.

Walter, Mildred Pitts. *Justin and the Best Biscuits in the World*. Illustrated by Catherine Stock. Lothrop, Lee & Shepard, 1986.

Watkins, Yoko Kawashima. *So Far from the Bamboo Grove*. Puffin, 1987.

Watson, James. *No Surrender*. HarperCollins, 1992.

Whelan, Gloria. *Goodbye Vietnam*. Knopf, 1992.

Wojciechowska, Maia. *Shadow of a Bull*. Aladdin, 1992.

Yee, Paul. *The Curses of Third Uncle*. Lorimer, 1986.

Yep, Laurence. *Child of the Owl*. Dell, 1978.

Yep, Laurence. *Dragonwings*. Harper Trophy, 1977.

Yep, Laurence. *The Lost Garden*. Julian Messner, 1991.

Yep, Laurence. *The Serpent's Children*. Harper & Row, 1984.

Yep, Laurence. *Star Fisher*. Puffin, 1992.

Zei, Alki. *Petros' War*. Translated from the Greek by Edward Fenton. Dutton, 1972.

Picture Books

Adoff, Arnold. *Black Is Brown Is Tan*. Harper & Row, 1973.

Andrews, Jan. *Very Last First Time*. Illustrated by Ian Wallace. Groundwood, 1985.

Armstrong, Jeannette. *Neekna and Chemai*. Theytus Books, 1983.

Bear, Glecia. *Two Little Girls Lost in the Bush: A Cree Story for Children*. Edited and Translated by Freda Ahenakew and H.C. Wolfart. Illustrated by Jerry Whitehead. Fifth House, 1991.

Bunting, Eve. *Fly Away Home*. Illustrated by Ronald Himler. Clarion, 1991.

Bunting, Eve. *The Happy Funeral*. Illustrated by Vo-Dinh Mai. Harper & Row, 1982.

Carrier, Roch. *The Boxing Match*. Illustrated by Sheldon Cohen. Translated from the French by Sheila Fischman. Tundra, 1991.

Carrier, Roch. *The Hockey Sweater*. Illustrated by Sheldon Cohen. Translated from the French by Sheila Fischman. Tundra, 1979.

Clifton, Lucille. *The Boy Who Didn't Believe in Spring*. Illustrated by Brinton Turkle. Dutton, 1988.

Clifton, Lucille. *Everett Anderson's Goodbye*. Illustrated by Ann Grifalconi. Holt, 1983.

Clifton, Lucille. *Everett Anderson's Nine Month Long*. Illustrated by Ann Grifalconi. Holt, 1978.

Cohen, Barbara. *The Carp in the Bathtub*. Illustrated by Joan Halpern. Lothrop, Lee & Shepard, 1972.

Dahl, Roald. *Roald Dahl's Revolting Rhymes*. Illustrated by Quentin Blake. Knopf, 1983.

Drucker, Malka. *Grandma's Latkes*. Illustrated by Eve Chwast. Harcourt Brace Jovanovich, 1992.

Flournoy, Valerie. *The Patchwork Quilt*. Illustrated by Jerry Pinkney. Dial, 1985.

French, Fiona. *Snow White in New York*. Oxford, 1987.

Gale, Donald. *Sooshewan: Child of the Beothuk*. Illustrated by Shawn Steffler. Breakwater, 1988.

Gallaz, Christophe. *Rose Blanche*. Illustrated by Roberto Innocenti. Creative Education, 1985.

Garland, Sherry. *The Lotus Seed*. Illustrated by Tatsuro Kluchi. Harcourt, 1993.

Grifalconi, Ann. *The Village of Round and Square Houses*. Little, Brown, 1986.

Hale, Sarah Josepha. *Mary Had a Little Lamb*. Photographs by Bruce McMillan. Scholastic, 1990.

Hewitt, Kathryn (reteller). *The Three Sillies*. Harcourt Brace Jovanovich, 1986.

Hughes, Monica. *A Handful of Seeds*. Paintings by Luis Garay. UNICEF Canada/Lester, 1993.

Isadora, Rachel. *At the Crossroads*. Greenwillow, 1991.

Isadora, Rachel. *Over the Green Hills*. Greenwillow, 1992.

King, Thomas. *A Coyote Columbus Story*. Pictures by William Kent Monkman. Groundwood, 1992.

Kusugak, Michael Arvaarluk. *Baseball Bats for Christmas*. Art by Vladyana Krykorka. Annick, 1991.

Kusugak, Michael Arvaarluk. *Hide and Sneak*. Art by Vladyana Krykorka. Annick, 1992.

Lawson, Julie. *The Dragon's Pearl*. Illustrated by Paul Morin. Oxford, 1992. Clarion, 1993.

Leaf, Margaret. *Eyes of the Dragon*. Illustrated by Ed Young. Lothrop, Lee & Shepard, 1987.

Lee, Jeannie M. *Ba' Nam*. Holt, 1987.

Lehtinen, Ritva. *The Grandchildren of the Incas*. Carolrhoda, 1992.

Levine, Ellen. *I Hate English!* Illustrated by Steve Björkman. Scholastic, 1989.

Levinson, Riki. *Our Home Is the Sea*. Illustrated by Dennis Luzak. Dutton, 1988.

Little, Jean, and Maggie DeVries. *Once Upon a Golden Apple*. Penguin, 1991.

Margolies, Barbara A. *Kanu of Kathmandu; A Journey in Nepal*. Four Winds, 1992.

Markun, Patricia Maloney. *The Little Painter of Sabana Grande*. Illustrated by Robert Casilla. Bradbury, 1993.

McKissack, Patricia. *Flossie and the Fox*. Illustrated by Rachel Isadora. Dial, 1986.

McKissack, Patricia. *Mirandy and Brother Wind*. Illustrated by Jerry Pinkney. Knopf, 1988.

McMahon, Patricia. *Chi-Hoon; A Korean Girl*. Photographs by Michael F. O'Brien. Caroline House, 1993.

Morimoto, Junko. *My Hiroshima*. Translated and adapted into English by Isao Morimoto and Anne Bower Ingram. Viking, 1990.

Morris, Ann. *Bread, Bread, Bread*. Photography by Ken Heyman. Mulberry, 1989.

Morris, Ann. *Hats, Hats, Hats*. Photography by Ken Heyman. Mulberry, 1989.

Munsch, Robert, and Michael Kusugak. *A Promise Is a Promise*. Illustrated by Vladyana Krykorka. Annick, 1988.

Musgrove, Margaret. *Ashanti to Zulu; African Traditions*. Pictures by Leo and Diane Dillon. Dial, 1976.

Nomura, Takaaki. *Grandpa's Town*. Translated from the Japanese by Amanda Mayer Stinchecum. Kane/Miller, 1991.

Perlman, Janet (reteller & adaptor). *Cinderella Penguin, or, The Little Glass Flipper*. Retold and illustrated by Janet Perlman. Kids Can, 1992.

Peters, Russell M. *Clambake; A Wampanoag Tradition*. Photographs by John Madama. Lerner, 1992.

Pinkney, Gloria Jean. *Back Home*. Illustrated by Jerry Pinkney. Dial, 1992.

Pitkänen, Matti A., with Reijo Härkönen. *The Children of China*. Carolrhoda, 1990.

Pitkänen, Matti A., with Reijo Härkönen. *The Children of Egypt*. Carolrhoda, 1991.

Pitkänen, Matti A., with Reijo Härkönen. *The Children of Nepal.* Carolrhoda, 1990.

Regguinti, Gordon. *The Sacred Harvest; Ojibway Wild Rice Gathering.* Photographs by Dale Kakkak. Lerner, 1992.

Ringgold, Faith. *Aunt Harriet's Underground Railroad in the Sky.* Crown, 1993.

Ringgold, Faith. *Tar Beach.* Crown, 1991.

Rylant, Cynthia. *Appalachia; The Voices of Sleeping Birds.* Illustrated by Barry Moser. Harcourt Brace Jovanovich, 1991.

Say, Allen. *The Bicycle Man.* Parnassus, 1982.

Say, Allen. *El Chino.* Houghton Mifflin, 1990.

Say, Allen. *Tree of Cranes.* Houghton Mifflin, 1991.

Scieszka, Jon. *The Frog Prince Continued.* Paintings by Steve Johnson. Viking, 1991.

Scieszka, Jon. *The Stinky Cheese Man: And Other Fairly Stupid Tales.* Illustrated by Lane Smith. Viking, 1992.

Scieszka, Jon. *The True Story of the Three Little Pigs* by A. Wolf. Illustrated by Lane Smith. Viking, 1989.

Steptoe, John. *Stevie.* Harper & Row, 1969.

Stevens, Janet (reteller). *The Three Billy Goats Gruff.* Harcourt Brace Jovanovich, 1987.

Surat, Michele Maria. *Angel Child, Dragon Child.* Pictures by Vo-Dinh Mai. Steck-Vaughn, 1992.

Swentzell, Rina. *Children of Clay; A Family of Pueblo Potters.* Photography by Bill Steen. Lerner, 1992.

Wallace, Ian. *Chin Chiang and the Dragon's Dance.* Groundwood, 1984.

Walter, Mildred Pitts. *Brother to the Wind.* Illustrated by Leo and Diane Dillon. Lothrop, Lee & Shepard, 1985.

Waters, Kate, and Madeline Slovenz-Low. *Lion Dancer; Ernie Wan's Chinese New Year.* Photographs by Martha Cooper. Scholastic, 1990.

Wheeler, Bernelda. *A Friend Called "Chum."* Illustrated by Andy Stout. Pemmican, 1984.

Wheeler, Bernelda. *I Can't Have Bannock, but the Beaver Has a Dam.* Illustrated by Herman Bekkering. Pemmican, 1984.

Wheeler, Bernelda. *Where Did You Get Your Moccasins?* Illustrated by Herman Bekkering. Pemmican, 1986.

Williams, Jay. *Everyone Knows What a Dragon Looks Like.* Illustrated by Mercer Mayer. Four Winds, 1976.

Williams, Karen Lynn. *Galimoto*. Illustrated by Catherine Stock. Lothrop, Lee & Shepard, 1990.

Yolen, Jane. *Encounter*. Illustrated by David Shannon. Harcourt Brace Jovanovich, 1992.

Yolen, Jane. *Sleeping Ugly*. Illustrated by Diane Stanley. Coward-McCann, 1981.

Folktales

Aardema, Verna (reteller). *Why Mosquitos Buzz in People's Ears: A West African Tale*. Illustrated by Leo and Diane Dillon. Puffin, 1993.

Alexander, Lloyd. *The Fortune Tellers*. Illustrated by Trina Schart Hyman. Dutton, 1992.

Bailey, Lydia. *Mei Ming and the Dragon's Daughter*. Illustrated by Martin Springett. Scholastic, 1990.

Bang, Molly. *Dawn*. Mulberry, 1991.

Bierhorst, John. *The Monkey's Haircut and Other Stories Told by the Maya*. Illustrated by Robert Andrew Parker. Morrow, 1986.

Bryan, Ashley. *The Cat's Purr*. Atheneum, 1985.

Cleaver, Elizabeth. *The Miraculous Hind, A Hungarian Legend*. Holt, 1973.

Cohlene, Terri (adaptor). *Clamshell Boy; A Makah Legend*. Illustrated by Charles Reasoner. Watermill Press, 1990.

Compton, Patricia A. (reteller). *The Terrible EEK*. Illustrated by Sheila Hamanaka. Simon & Schuster, 1991.

Demi. *The Empty Pot*. Holt, 1990.

Gilman, Phoebe. *Something from Nothing*. North Winds, 1992.

Goble, Paul. *Love Flute*. Bradbury, 1992.

Hamilton, Virginia. *The All Jahdu Storybook*. Harcourt Brace Jovanovich, 1991.

Hamilton, Virginia. *The Dark Way, Stories from the Spirit World*. Illustrated by Lambert Davis. Harcourt Brace Jovanovich, 1990.

Hamilton, Virginia (reteller). *The People Could Fly; American Black Folktales*. Illustrated by Leo and Diane Dillon. Knopf, 1993.

Harris, Joel Chandler. *Jump Again! More Adventures of Brer Rabbit*. Adapted by Van Dyke Parks. Illustrated by Barry Moser. Harcourt Brace Jovanovich, 1987.

Hearn, Lafcadio. *The Voice of the Great Bell*. Retold by Margaret Hodges. Illustrated by Ed Young. Little, Brown, 1989.

Heyer, Marilee. *The Weaving of a Dream*. Viking, 1986.

Hooks, William H. *Moss Gown*. Illustrated by Donald Carrick. Clarion, 1987.

Hughes, Monica. *Little Fingerling*. Illustrated by Brenda Clark. Kids Can, 1989.

Ishii, Momoko (reteller). *The Tongue-cut Sparrow*. Translated from the Japanese by Katherine Paterson. Illustrated by Suekichi Akaba. Lodestar, 1987.

Jaquith, Priscilla (reteller). *Bo Rabbit Smart for True; Folktales from the Gullah*. Drawings by Ed Young. Philomel, 1981.

Johnson, Ryerson. *Kenji and the Magic Geese*. Illustrated by Jean and Mou-sien Tseng. Simon & Schuster, 1992.

Louie, Ai-Ling (reteller). *Yeh-Shen; A Cinderella Story from China*. Illustrated by Ed Young. Philomel, 1982.

Martin, Rafe. *The Rough-Face Girl*. Illustrated by David Shannon. Putnam's, 1992.

McDermott, Gerald. *Zomo the Rabbit; A Trickster Tale from West Africa*. Harcourt Brace Jovanovich, 1992.

Mollel, Tololwa M. *The King and the Tortoise*. Illustrated by Kathy Blankley. Lester, 1993.

Mollel, Tololwa M. *The Orphan Boy*. Illustrated by Paul Morin. Clarion, 1991.

Morris, Winifred. *The Future of Yen-Tzu*. Illustrated by Friso Henstra. Atheneum, 1992.

Muller, Robin. *The Magic Paintbrush*. Doubleday, 1989.

Nunes, Susan (reteller). *Tiddalick, the Frog*. Illustrated by Ju-Hong Chen. Atheneum, 1989.

Okanagan Tribal Council. *How Food Was Given*. 1984.

Okanagan Tribal Council. *How Names Were Given*. 1984.

Okanagan Tribal Council. *How Turtle Set the Animals Free*. 1984.

Paterson, Katherine (translator). *The Tale of the Mandarin Ducks*. Illustrated by Leo and Diane Dillon. Dutton, 1990.

Rosen, Michael. *How the Animals Got Their Colors*. Illustrated by John Clementson. Lester, 1992.

Rossetti, Bernadette (translator and reteller). *Musdzi 'Udada/The Owl*. Dene Language Institute, 1991.

San Souci, Robert D. *Sukey and the Mermaid*. Illustrated by Brian Pinkney. Four Winds, 1992.

Scribe, Murdo. *Murdo's Story: A Legend from Northern Manitoba*. Illustrated by Terry Gallagher. Pemmican, 1992.

Shetterly, Susan Hand. *The Dwarf-Wizard of Uxmal*. Illustrated by Robert Shetterly. Atheneum, 1990.

Spray, Carole. *The Mare's Egg: A New World Folk Tale*. Illustrated by Kim LaFave. Camden House, 1981.

Steptoe, John. *Mufaro's Beautiful Daughters*. Lothrop, Lee & Shepard, 1987.

Steptoe, John. *The Story of Jumping Mouse; A Native American Legend*. Lothrop, Lee & Shepard, 1984.

Stevens, Janet (reteller). *Coyote Steals the Blanket; A Ute Tale*. Holiday House, 1993.

Tan, Amy. *The Moon Lady*. Illustrated by Gretchen Schields. Macmillan, 1992.

Taylor, C. J. *The Ghost and Lone Warrior*. Tundra, 1991.

Taylor, C. J. *How Two-Feather Was Saved from Loneliness*. Tundra, 1990.

Taylor, C. J. *Little Water and the Gift of the Animals*. Tundra, 1992.

Te Kanawa, Kiri. *Land of the Long White Cloud; Maori Myths, Tales and Legends*. Illustrated by Michael Foreman. Arcade, 1989.

Toye, William (reteller). *How Summer Came to Canada*. Illustrated by Elizabeth Cleaver. Oxford, 1969.

Toye, William (reteller). *The Loon's Neckace*. Illustrated by Elizabeth Cleaver. Oxford, 1969.

Toye, William (reteller). *The Mountain Goats of Temlaham*. Illustrated by Elizabeth Cleaver. Oxford, 1969.

Vuong, Lynette Dyer. *The Brocaded Slipper and Other Vietnamese Tales*. Illustrated by Vo-Dinh Mai. HarperCollins, 1992.

Watkins, Yoko Kawashima. *Tales from the Bamboo Grove*. Illustrations by Jean and Mou-sien Tseng. Bradbury, 1992.

Wolkstein, Diane. *The Magic Wings: A Tale from China*. Dutton, 1983.

Wolkstein, Diane. *White Wave: A Chinese Tale*. Illustrated by Ed Young. Crowell, 1979.

Yacowitz, Caryn (adaptor). *The Jade Stone; A Chinese Folktale*. Illustrated by Ju-Hong Chen. Holiday House, 1992.

Yee, Paul. *Tales from Gold Mountain; Stories of the Chinese in the New World*. Illustrated by Simon Ng. Groundwood, 1989.

Yep, Laurence. *The Rainbow People*. Harper & Row, 1989.

Yolen, Jane. *The Emperor and the Kite*. Illustrated by Ed Young. Philomel, 1988.

Young, Ed. *Lon Po Po; A Red-Riding Hood Story from China*. Philomel, 1989.

Poetry

Bouchard, David. *The Elders Are Watching*. Illustrated by Roy Henry Vickers. Eagle Dancer Enterprises, 1990.

Bryan, Ashley. *Sing to the Sun*. HarperCollins, 1992.

Bryan, Ashley (selector). *All Night, All Day: A Child's First Book of African-American Sprituals*. Atheneum, 1991.

Cendrars, Blaise. *Shadow*. Illustrated and translated by Marcia Brown. Scribner's, 1982.

George, Chief Dan. *My Heart Soars*. Hancock House, 1989.

Mado, Michio. *The Animals; Selected Poems*. Decorations by Mitsumasa Anno. Translated by The Empress Michiko of Japan. McElderry, 1992.

Nye, Naomi Shihab. *This Same Sky; A Collection of Poems from Around the World*. Four Winds, 1992.

*Editions of *Cricket Magazine*.

Publishing Acknowledgements

Every effort has been made to acknowledge all sources of material used in this book. The publisher would be grateful if any errors or omissions were pointed out, so that they may be corrected.

From *A Jar of Dreams* by Yoshiko Uchida. McElderry, 1981.

From *Park's Quest* by Catherine Paterson. Lodestar, 1988.

From *Shabanu, Daughter of the Wind* by Suzanne Fisher Staples. Knopf, 1989.

From *Stepping on the Cracks* by Mary Downing Hahn. Clarion, 1991.

From *The Curses of Third Uncle* by Paul Yee. Lorimer, 1986.

From *The Eternal Spring of Mr. Ito* by Sheila Garrigue. Bradbury, 1985.

From *Star Fisher* by Laurence Yep. Morrow, 1991.

From *Tikta'liktak* by James Houston. Longmans, 1965.

From *Underground to Canada* by Barbara Smucker. Irwin, 1977.

From *Year of Impossible Goodbyes* by Sook Nyul Choi. Houghton Mifflin, 1991.

From *School Library Journal*. September & November 1991.